'Since the light bulb of understanding God ___ Marcus's head I have seen it transform his attitude to life and ministry. His enthusiasm to help others grasp this reality and live with true joy is infectious.'
Nigel D. Pollock, National Director, Tertiary Students Christian Fellowship, New Zealand

'A precise and life-transforming book that is well founded in Scripture. It speaks straight into the human heart, and to all cultures, languages and nations. This is a courageous piece of work that avoids ambiguity when it comes to finding joy.'
Peter Oyugi, Director of Students' Ministry, FOCUS-Kenya

'Marcus is right to say that there is a lack of genuine joy in many Christians today. His analysis that this is merely a symptom of a far more fundamental problem of not really understanding and believing some of the greatest truths of the gospel is vitally important. All Christians need to hear Marcus's message and rediscover the great truths, like grace, that lie at the heart of the gospel.'
Michael You, Tutor, Associate Programme, St Helen's Church, Bishopsgate, London

'Coming to faith in the Lord Jesus Christ is entirely by God's grace; that's clear! Sadly, many of us quickly revert to *living* by works, not grace. No wonder, says Marcus Honeysett, that we rapidly lose our joy in Christ. This book is all about radical life-in-grace, and the joy that flows from that. Questions at the end of each chapter, for personal or group use, reinforce Honeysett's thesis, drawn from careful study of New Testament material. An arresting and heart-warming read.'
Rose Dowsett, International Conference and Training Minister, OMF International

'Marcus's book is an extremely helpful look at an issue of fundamental importance to our faith. It's engaging, stimulating, liberating and deeply refreshing.'
Tony Watkins, Managing Editor, CultureWatch

'It is vital to grasp that Christians are under grace and not law because it is critical for our joy. This is a truth that Marcus has grasped and explained in a way faithful to Scripture. He has done so in an easy-to-read and uplifting style. I wish this book had been around when he and I worked together, and the words on the lips of many Christian workers were "I am tired".'

Wanyeki Mahiaini, Co-ordinator of the Philip Project, training preachers for Africa

Finding Joy

A radical rediscovery of grace

Marcus Honeysett

ivp

Inter-Varsity Press

INTER-VARSITY PRESS
38 De Montfort Street, Leicester LE1 7GP, *England*
Email: ivp@uccf.org.uk
Website: www.ivpbooks.com

First published 2005

British Library Cataloguing in Publication Data
A catalogue record for this book is available from the British Library.

ISBN-13: 978-1-84474-086-4
ISBN-10: 1-84474-086-2

Set in Dante 10.5/13pt
Typeset in Great Britain by CRB Associates, Reepham, Norfolk
Printed and bound in Great Britain by Creative Print and Design (Wales),
Ebbw Vale

Inter-Varsity Press is the publishing division of the Universities and
Colleges Christian Fellowship (formerly the Inter-Varsity Fellowship),
a student movement linking Christian Unions in universities and
colleges throughout Great Britain, and a member movement of the
International Fellowship of Evangelical Students. For more information
about local and national activities write to UCCF, 38 De Montfort Street,
Leicester LE1 7GP, *email us at email@uccf.org.uk, or visit the UCCF*
website at www.uccf.org.uk.

Contents

Acknowledgments

A big thank-you to the friends and team members who have encouraged me to write. Many have commented on all or part of the manuscript and it is much better for their kind work. Special thanks to all the team at IVP and to Derek Baldwin for his incredibly detailed and helpful comments. All errors are, of course, mine.

My thanks also go to those who have encouraged me to grow in my grasp of grace and joy – especially Cassells Morel, Derek Cross and Dr J. Piper, whose books and sermons have influenced me greatly.

And to Ros, for consistent encouragement, patience and love. A wife of noble character is worth more than rubies and her husband lacks nothing of value.

Introduction

Outside the window a light dusting of snow fell silently as the evening shadows crept up the mountainside. The ski resort had an air of jollity, the bars were full, smiling faces in the restaurants. It was Christmas Eve.

Inside the hotel a party of Christians were celebrating Christmas. Later in the evening we would be out carol singing in the streets and telling the amazing message of Christmas to anyone who would listen. But first we were praising God together and listening to the Bible. My evening message that day was taken from the letter the apostle Paul wrote to the church in Philippi. In Philippians 4:4 he exhorts and encourages his readers to rejoice in the Lord. To enjoy God, to express to him the delight and overflowing joy that they know in their relationship with him. So thrilled is Paul with this theme that he repeats it: 'Rejoice in the Lord always. I will say it again: Rejoice!'

Philippians is a letter loaded and overflowing with joy. Paul says in 3:1:

> Finally, my brothers, rejoice in the Lord! It is no trouble for me to write the same things to you again, and it is a safeguard for you.

He wants to remind them continually of the great treasure they have in Jesus. He expects that as they enjoy Christ their growing faith will protect them from false religion and from settling for less than God has for them.

As we looked through the whole letter to the Philippians in the mountain hotel that week, the theme of joy came up again and again. Philippians 1:25–26 describes the experience of a genuine relationship with Jesus. Paul tells his readers that he wants them to grow as Christians and to know and experience overflowing joy in Christ.

Over dinner, following the praise and preaching, a member of the party asked if he could talk to me.

'I've read through Philippians this week,' he said, 'and see a great deal of joy in this letter. Even in prison Paul was clearly enthralled by Jesus Christ and wanted the Philippians to have the kind of deep enjoyment of their faith that he did.'

'That's clearly one of the big purposes of the letter,' I agreed.

'But my problem is this,' he continued. 'I can see a lot of joy here in the Bible, but frankly I can't see anything like it in my life. So what's wrong? How do I get it?'

That question, or one like it, was repeated again and again by others that week, as we pored over the Bible together and heard it speaking about a depth and richness of Christian life that did not sit comfortably with a lot of our current experience:

- 'I have trusted Jesus. He has forgiven my sins. Is that the extent of my Christian life, or should I expect more than that?'
- 'Doesn't the Bible teach that this world is fallen and full of sin and pain, and that heaven is where we experience joy?'
- 'Isn't the vocabulary of joy and enjoying God just a Christianized reflection of our hedonistic age that only wants personal comfort and happiness?'
- 'The Bible tells me that Christians are slaves of Christ. Surely that speaks about duty rather than enjoyment. My aim should be to serve and obey rather than to enjoy.'
- 'Isn't enjoyment far too subjective and emotional to describe our objective state before God? Doesn't it smack of me working myself up to feel good, rather than dwelling on mighty and weighty truths?'

These questions are the reason for this book. As I talked with people who came with questions about Philippians and about Christian living, I often felt a fraud. They expressed the tension I feel in my own life, that my experience of the grace of the Lord Jesus, my delight in my salvation and my joy in the gospel are often not as I think they should be, or as the Bible describes. The question of my friends 'So what is going wrong?' is also my question. I am not writing this book as someone who has arrived.

Whenever I found myself in a conversation about feeling joyless in comparison with the description of the Christian life in Philippians, I asked the following questions to try to get some kind of handle on what I was hearing:

1. Why do you read the Bible?
2. Do you ever take deliberate or regular time to adore Christ?
3. Would you say that you prioritize the kinds of things in your life Paul obviously rejoices over in Philippians, and seems to want others to take joy in?
4. How would you describe your worship life?
5. Can you describe what God is doing in your life at the moment?

I received very similar answers from almost everybody I talked to. They were all Christians who wanted to love and obey the Lord, and attended churches where the Bible is well taught. Here is how they responded:

1. Most said they read the Bible in order to understand God better. In several cases they added that they read the Bible for understanding in order that they can serve God more faithfully.
2. When asked if they took regular or deliberate time to adore God and his Christ, most admitted they didn't.
3. When asked whether Paul's priorities were their own, many confessed that the practical *application* of the Bible was the thing they found most difficult in the Christian life. Many identified that they can hear a spellbinding sermon, be satisfied that they have discovered *what* the Bible says and *how* it says it, but struggle to *do* it, or to make the Christian experience they read about their own.

4. When asked about their worship life, I received two different answers. One set of people reacted strongly against the use of the word 'worship' being used in connection with emotion, or religious affections, or individual and corporate prayer and singing. An oft-repeated sentence was 'Worship has nothing to do with my emotions: it is the whole of my life of obedience to the truth, lived out before God.' The other set of answers identified worship almost entirely with corporate singing on the one hand, and (almost contradictorily) with highly individualized emotional response to God on the other.

5. When asked if they could identify what God was doing in their lives at the moment, an alarming number of people simply thought the question was irrelevant. A lot more thought it should be relevant but had no idea how to answer. Several people told me that nobody had ever asked them before.

All of this made me think about what the gospel has to say about these reflections.

Glorious good news

The gospel is God's wonderful saving message about his Son, Jesus Christ. God made the world very good. He created people as the high point, made in his image, bearing his stamp and imprint. God made us with the ability to make moral choices with real consequences, and he did so fully aware that the primary choice made by the first people, Adam and Eve, would be to deny his rule and try to enthrone themselves. This rebellion by Adam and Eve, and subsequently in all people, is what the Bible describes as 'sin'. The rebellion of people against God twisted the whole created order. However beautiful and magnificent that order is, at root it became flawed, rebellious and anti-God. Or, to put it the Bible's way, it was cursed by God (Genesis 3:17).

However, right from the start God has always planned to have a people rescued from the curse by his Son. The cross of Jesus Christ is the most important event in history. Jesus willingly died to take the punishment humans deserve for rebellion and diverted the anger of God away from us and on to himself. Therefore we can now receive every blessing of God because of him. We don't deserve any blessings, but God gives them freely to all who put their trust in Jesus and his saving death. That is what the Bible calls 'grace'. The grace of Christ is at the very heart of the good news.

Christian joy is the experience of gladness or happiness, not in plans or possessions or people, but *in God*. God is delighted to save sinners: he invites us into a relationship with him in which he gives that joy to us. This means that if we are unable to identify anything in our lives that looks like New Testament joy, or if we never resonate with the command to rejoice in the Lord, we are right to ask whether something is wrong. As we talked about Philippians, one man said to me, 'Are you not just trying to emotionalize Christian faith? I've never known anything like that, are you saying my Christian life is deficient?' I was deeply uneasy for him. I believe that anyone who can put into words that he has never felt joy in the Lord and doesn't think there is anything wrong with this is out of sync with the biblical picture of normal Christian living.

Reasons for joylessness

Why might Christians have lost the joy of salvation or know no delight in the Lord? I can think of several possibilities. It could be that they have been through exhausting times, emotionally, spiritually or physically and have had the spiritual vitality drained from them by disappointments or heartache. They may have been through great pain and been bewildered about why God didn't seem to act to alleviate it. It could be that they have become Christians in an environment that has never encouraged them to rejoice in the Lord or that has portrayed the Christian life to be all duty and moral correctness. Maybe they have never been encouraged to worship or pray. It could be that they have never been encouraged to prioritize the things that the Bible says bring joy. It may even be that people aren't yet Christians, but have assumed they are. Whatever the reason, those who know a conspicuous lack of Christian joy are unlikely to find faith energizing, are unlikely to participate fully in the body of Christ, and are unlikely to make any impact on the world.

Joy and grace

This is a book about joy and grace. I am convinced that many Christians struggle with joylessness because they do not really trust that the gospel is the good news of God's grace. Instead they believe that the Christian life is about performing religious duty to be good enough for God or to express gratitude to him for salvation. I believe that many more struggle with joylessness because they do not make priorities out of things the Bible says bring us joy.

The first part of this book looks at how the joy of the first-century church in Galatia was crippled by legalism and religious duty and how Paul urged them to recover their delight in God. The second part explores some of the blessings of God's grace the Bible tells us will bring joy, if only we will live in them.

Since my trip to the mountains, I have taught Philippians in many other places. Maybe you resonate with the repeated question 'How do you get the joy Paul talks about, which I know so little about?' That is the theme of this book. I pray that it might play a small part in helping you believe the good news of the grace of God. I hope that it might encourage you to discern biblical priorities for you to make your own and that it might encourage you to love God with all your heart and soul and mind and strength.

Part 1
Finding joy through grace

1 How to believe the gospel of grace

As contestants step up to the famous black chair on TV's *Mastermind*, the lights dim, the audience goes silent and the quizmaster tersely asks them their name, occupation and specialist subject as a way of categorizing each participant. We enjoy the spectacle as they face two minutes of questions with beads of sweat pouring down their faces.

We often like to categorize people in order to get a handle on who they are. If you start studies at a university or college, the first question everyone will ask you is, 'What A levels did you do?' They want to know if you might have anything in common with them. A recent television programme asked several celebrities 'Who are you?' in relation to their family history, the idea being that your family tree holds important clues to your identity.

How do you normally answer the question 'Who are you?'

People describe their identity in different ways. Many understand themselves primarily in terms of what they do for an occupation. Others think of themselves in terms of what they have or what they experience. Others define themselves in terms of their relationships. And still others by their aspirations, ambitions or by what they eat.

In the letter to the Galatians, the apostle Paul says that Christians have a supernatural identity:

But when the time had fully come, God sent his Son, born of a woman, born under law, to redeem those under law, that we might receive the full rights of sons. Because you are sons, God sent the Spirit of his Son into our hearts, the Spirit who calls out, 'Abba, Father.' So you are no longer a slave, but a son; and since you are a son, God has made you also an heir. (Galatians 4:4–7)

These are dynamic verses that all Christians should commit to memory and rejoice over. They go straight to the heart of who we are. (The use of 'son' may sound sexist, but it isn't, because it is the Bible's language for being an heir.) Christians are a different kind of people. God has changed our identity from being slaves to being his children. When we are asked to describe ourselves, some of the first things to come to a Christian's mind should be *I am a son of God*; *I am an heir of life*; *I am someone in whom God's Spirit lives*; *I am a child of the King*; *I bear the family likeness*. All of these things should make joy well up inside us, making us want to worship and revel in God and our salvation. God has done all these transforming things for us. He sent his Son. He sent his Holy Spirit, the Spirit who cries from inside us to the Father. He makes us sons and heirs. It is all from him, it is all given us through grace.

Grace forgotten
Sadly this grace wasn't being received and remembered in the churches in Galatia. The problem in Galatia was that they had forgotten the gospel of grace. They had failed to keep in mind their status before God, in Jesus. As a result they had reverted to Old Testament ways of religion, believing that the Christian life is not about receiving grace, but about performing religious activities for God's pleasure. Paul calls this 'living under the law' and is passionately opposed to it because it is the ultimate grace-blocker. He goes so far as to say it is actually 'another gospel' (Galatians 1:7), which isn't good news at all, but bad news. Such bad news, in fact, that anyone who spreads it is worthy of God's condemnation (1:9).

How to kill joy
A major consequence for the Galatians of trusting a message of law and works was that all their joy had gone (Galatians 4:15). When they

first received the true good news of grace, they were filled with joy. However, when false teachers came into the church and started to preach that people should now continue their relationship with the Lord by working hard at performance of religious duty, the joy disappeared. It is not hard to see why. At first they knew all the blessings of being united to Jesus, freely given to them by God. Then they were told that to continue enjoying God they had to work hard for a human righteousness that is, in fact, unattainable.

Joylessness is often an indicator that we have forgotten the gospel of God's grace and are turning instead to legalism. I will use the words 'legalism' and 'law' to refer to two slightly different things in this book, both of which Christians must avoid. The first is the idea that we can judge the success of our Christian lives by how faithfully we keep the law that God gave to Israel in the Old Testament. I am convinced that the New Testament tells us that law-keeping is impossible, that only Jesus could keep God's commands and that he did so on our behalf. We can never measure how well we are doing as Christians by whether we are keeping the law or not.

The second, related, way I refer to legalism or law is the attempt to measure our Christian life by *any* kind of religious performance or duty. Churches so often seem to be full of good people doing good things and it can be all too easy to reason that growing as a Christian means working hard at being good and doing good activities. Faithfulness is translated as duty, Christian experience transmutes into Christian activity, and love for the Lord can easily degenerate into fulfilling the expectations the church has for our behaviour: 'Don't go there. Don't wear those clothes. Don't drink that ... ' One man recently said to me, 'Worship is nothing more than me offering all my deeds as acts of dutiful obedience to God.' He is wrong. Saying to God 'I do these things for you because it is my duty to do them' does not honour him. Worship that is mere duty is no worship at all. If we believe that worship is duty, then we have forgotten the good news of grace and have put ourselves under law. Trusting our performance of works to make ourselves right with God robs us of our joy in him.

Receiving grace
What does it look like to receive and live in grace? And what exactly is the connection between grace and joy? Romans 5 describes authentic

Christian living as 'reigning in life' (Romans 5:17). Reigning in life sounds great, but our natural tendency can often be to define it by what we *do*. 'I reign in life by how well I can maintain my spiritual disciplines'; 'I reign in life by attending church twice on a Sunday and once in the week'; 'I reign in life when I am persuaded that my Bible reading and prayer times are long enough.' A friend once asked me, 'Am I right in thinking that the only real measure of a successful spiritual life is how often I can read the Bible?' We can see how easy a trap that is to fall into. Reading the Bible is an excellent and vital thing for Christians to do. It is the only way God has promised to speak. My friend, however, thought that the frequency of his dutiful activity, rather than meeting with God, was the key factor in determining the success of his Christian life.

'Is this approach to Christian living working for you?' I asked.

'If I am being honest, it isn't really,' he replied. 'But I'm not sure why.'

'When did you last have a good time with the Lord when reading the Bible?'

'Ages ago. Months ago. I do it every day and I'm learning a lot of facts. I do get quite enthusiastic when I see how verses work or bits of the Bible hang together.'

'Do you think that's sufficient?' I questioned.

'Not really. I don't understand how my brain can be stimulated but I can still feel spiritually empty. After all, I'm doing the disciplined study. Isn't that meant to give me a fulfilled Christian life?'

My friend's problem was that he had confused how the Bible *works* with knowing God through the Bible. He was therefore (sometimes) excited when his logic comprehended some point of meaning. However, what he was really keen on was not the Lord, but study. Study can often be very helpful, but it is dangerously misleading to believe that the quality of our Bible study (or any other Christian work) is the measure of our relationship with God. It is a way to replace receiving grace with doing activities.

Reigning in life

Romans 5:17 tells us how Christians reign in life:

> For if, by the trespass of the one man, death reigned through that one

man, how much more will those who receive God's abundant provision
of grace and of the gift of righteousness reign in life through the one
man, Jesus Christ.

(Romans 5:17)

It isn't by *doing* anything. It doesn't come through being moral or
by the regularity of our church attendance or our Bible study. We
reign by *receiving* something – the abundant provision of God's grace
and the gift of righteousness.

Reigning in life means that we are kings or queens in the presence
of God! Death is no longer the ruler, believers rule! Bible teacher John
Stott says about this verse:

> We become kings, sharing the kingship of Christ, with even death
> under our feet now, and one day to be destroyed.[1]

If you are reading this as a Christian believer, this is who you are –
a king! Jesus has made us kings and priests to serve God for ever. He
has poured out grace for us to receive. He has not given it in a stingy,
ungenerous way. He has given it in superabundance through Jesus. In
his first letter the apostle John says:

> How great is the love the Father has lavished on us, that we should be
> called children of God! And that is what we are!
> (1 John 3:1)

Some people can point to the moment when they became a
Christian. For others it happened as a slow process of dawning
realization that the good news is true and that Jesus is their Lord. But
for both kinds of believers, coming to that realization should, under
normal circumstances, be the spark that ignites joy in God as you
realize what you have become. Take verses like this:

> Therefore, since we have been justified through faith, we have peace
> with God through our Lord Jesus Christ, through whom we have
> gained access by faith into this grace in which we now stand. And
> we rejoice in the hope of the glory of God.
> (Romans 5:1–2)

Christians *have* been justified. We have already been declared right with God. Full stop. It is achieved. No sin or failure can ever alter that fact. When the Devil accuses a Christian before God he is doomed to disappointment.

Satan: God, you are holy. This person is a rebel. You *must* condemn and punish her.

God: My Son has died her death and suffered my wrath on her behalf.

Satan: She continues to sin. She is completely unworthy to enter your presence.

God: I made Jesus who had no sin to be sin for her, so that she might become the righteousness of God in him. The exchange is done.

Satan: Let there be payment from her in this life to make up for her crimes.

God: I declare her acquitted and righteous in Christ. There is now no condemnation for those who are in Christ Jesus. Nothing in all creation shall separate them from the love of God in Christ.

As a result we now live in grace and look forward with certain hope to the glory of God.

Express your joy

When Paul uses the word 'rejoice' in Romans 5 and elsewhere, we could translate it as 'enjoy', 'take enjoyment in' or 'delight in'. We don't use the word 'joy' very much today, but we do use the word 'enjoy'. Perhaps 'rejoice' has a bit more of an active connotation – 'give expression to your joy. Let your joy out!'

As a child I attended a church that behaved as though enthusiasm and reverence were mutually exclusive. If children whispered in church, it was almost a matter for church discipline. Hymns were sung 'reverently', which meant boringly. We turned off our enthusiasm switch at the door, and over the threshold was a place devoid of joy. Maybe you have been in similar places. It is a tragedy when Christians and churches forget or neglect to rejoice in the Lord. It reveals that we have advertently or inadvertently downgraded the value of being justified by faith and being declared by God to be acceptable in his presence.

As we read on in Romans 5, we discover other things to rejoice in. Things we are even *commanded* to rejoice in. It is not often in life that we are commanded to enjoy good things! Romans 5:11 says we rejoice in God through Jesus, and in our reconciliation. This means we should regularly bring God to mind and fall on our knees saying, 'God, in you I find the best joy and the most lasting satisfaction for my soul!' Romans 5:3 challengingly says we rejoice in suffering as Christians, because suffering for Jesus produces Jesus-like character in us, as we discover his love poured into our hearts by the Holy Spirit. There is blessing to enjoy, even through suffering.

Keep reminding yourself

We can easily stop reminding ourselves what it felt like the first time we grasped the reality of grace. Life bears in on us, there are many pressures, and all of a sudden it is possible to catch ourselves and realize that maybe we aren't expecting the same of God and aren't enjoying him as we once did. If we attend a church where grace isn't taught, then forgetting is all the easier.

A while ago I visited a church to preach about grace. Afterwards a man confessed to me he felt guilty every day for something he had done 50 years before. Every week for 50 years he had been in church, but he could not remember ever being taught about grace. He said, 'This grace thing sounds amazing, but why haven't I heard about it before?' Maybe he hadn't been listening, or maybe the church had neglected it. Whatever the reason, the reality of Jesus and the good news of his grace had been pushed to the margins of the man's mind. As a Christian his objective state was that he had peace with God and stood in grace, but he was never encouraged to believe it and was unable to enjoy it.

God gives his Son and every good thing to Christians. He doesn't do it because we are so lovely and deserving, but because he is so loving. He has blessed us with every spiritual blessing in Christ. Now you may not *feel* that way as you read this, but that is the reality. Christians have access, by faith in Jesus, into the riches of God's grace. Faith is not something we do. Faith is trusting God and receiving grace. Sometimes people say, 'I wish I had your faith,' which misunderstands faith, making it out to be a commodity or a work. They mean, 'If I can just work myself up to have enough of it, then

God compensates me in return when I reach a certain level of spiritual fervour.'

No! Faith is receiving. Faith is trusting God to do for you as he has promised. It isn't what *we* do. When you receive a birthday present you don't commend yourself because of the excellent way you receive it. Your act of receiving doesn't contribute anything to the present or the kindness of the giver. The same is true with faith, which starts by saying, 'God, I believe your promises and I trust that you want to give yourself to me.' When we do, we receive grace and reign in life, through Jesus Christ.

The Sunday-school definition of grace is 'God's Riches At Christ's Expense'. That is a pretty good definition. Grace is every good thing we don't deserve given to us by God because of Jesus Christ. Forgiveness, for example. You can't buy it or earn it – God offers it to you freely. All Christians have experienced it in their lives. We are adopted as God's sons, made co-heirs of heaven along with Jesus, by grace. We are seated in the heavenly realms, in Jesus, by grace. We are counting ourselves dead to sin and being empowered to reign in life, by grace. Christians have taken off the filthy rags of our own sordid attempts at being righteous and have been freely given royal white clothes, pure and guilt free, because of grace. Our lives are hidden with Christ in God. God delights in us and calls us his own because his grace is overflowing and free to sinners who admit their need.

Grace leads to joy

Grace is so wonderful that receiving it leads to joy as night follows day. It is impossible to taste something so delightful and not enjoy it and be stirred up to worship God.

Paul doesn't conclude with the blessings of grace we currently enjoy. Romans 5:2 says because of the good news we can also look to the future and enjoy what we are *going* to have in Christ, through grace. Literally he says we *boast* in the hope of the glory of God. Here is something worth boasting about: we are going to see and share God's glory one day. We have a down payment now, the Holy Spirit living in us. When we go to be with the Lord we will be completely and eternally wrapped in the glory of his majesty. This is certain, because it all depends on something already done – Jesus *has* won access to grace for us. Think about that today as you go about whatever you're doing. God's grace has enabled you to enter his presence for ever, not kneeling like a slave, but standing like a son. And we rejoice, even boast, in it.

Knowing and recognizing the truth of the good news must lead to us reckoning on it in our lives. We should be preaching it to ourselves every day. Characters in the Bible preach to their own hearts and souls. They say things like 'Why are you downcast, my soul? Put your hope in God!' That is preaching to our soul. It is saying, 'My heart – realize the reality of God's goodness. Fix your eyes on him; don't be distracted. Trust him and find him to be good. Worship him even if you aren't feeling like it, because he is worthy anyway.'

Let's preach every day to our hearts that we stand in the truth of God's grace. Let's consider it to be true about ourselves and be glad. This is who we are: grace people! It is our identity in Christ. Any distraction from this truth leads us away from who we are and away from the true good news, into bad news.

I remember being in a meeting with two colleagues from different churches. We opened the Bible to Philippians 3 and were considering what it meant to take joy in God. One of my colleagues said, 'I can honestly say that in the last six months I have known genuine Christian joy in my life for the first time.' We were excited by that and asked him what was making him joyful. He replied, 'I am often happy in worship on a Sunday, but it tends to be fleeting and leave me when I go to work on Monday. But in the last six months I have been strongly encouraged to get into the Bible. I am discovering that when your joy is based on the truth, and not just on feelings, it stays with you.' My other colleague responded thoughtfully, 'I am interested to hear you say that, because I too have recently been experiencing genuine and lasting joy for the first time. With me the difference has not been getting into the Bible, as I do that a great deal already. With me the difference has been applying the Bible to my life and actively expecting God to do things in me, and through me, by the Holy Spirit. And he has been.'

That was an exciting meeting! From very different perspectives my two friends were experiencing that knowing biblical truth, expecting God to work out the truth in us through the Holy Spirit, and Christian joy all go together. They were reflecting Romans 5 gospel living, rejoicing in the truth of the gospel and knowing the love of God in their hearts, by the Spirit.

I realized in that meeting that if we neglect either facet, then we are likely to forget about grace. It is no good to worship but not be firmly rooted in the truth of the Bible, because we won't know whether we are worshipping the true God or be able to say whether anything substantial underpins our happiness as we praise. But it is equally poor to read the Bible in a theoretical way that does not lead to worship and rejoicing in God. God's chief desire is that he is worshipped and glorified. When people read his word but don't translate it into worship, they are not acting as Christians. If we abandon either of these things our experience of grace may well end up either as wishy-washy and inaccurate or as purely theoretical. And where there is an inadequate grasp of grace there is no lasting joy in the Lord.

Questions

At the end of this chapter pause and ask yourself the following:

1. Read Romans 5:1–2. Memorize it.
2. Correct the following sentence:

   > Therefore since we have been justified by trying to be good, we have peace with God through our faithfulness. Through our activity we have gained access by faith into the church, and we expect to work hard for God because he commands it.

3. Read Galatians 4:5–6.

   - What is the status of people who were under the law, now that they have believed in Jesus?
   - What is the difference between a slave and a son?
   - What is the appropriate reaction this should produce in our hearts?

4. Which are you more likely to neglect: basing your faith on biblical truth or expecting to experience the work of the Holy Spirit in your life? Why?

Notes

1 John R. W. Stott, *The Message of Romans*, The Bible Speaks Today (IVP, 1994), p. 156.

The terrible tale of
2 legalism in Galatia

How do we know we are making progress in our Christian life? In other areas of life it is quite easy. With our health we can measure our pulse rate or cholesterol levels. With sporting achievements we can compare ourselves to others, win races, chalk up successes. In the business world we can achieve productivity targets or sales increases. But how do we measure progress in the Christian life? That was the question my friend in the last chapter asked. He concluded that, just as in society, successful Christian living is measured by performance and achievement – in his case the regularity of his Bible study.

It is easy to get lured into thinking in worldly terms of targets, promotions, and measures of activity. For example, surely there is a clear pecking order in churches, with the most successful Christians at the top? First is the vicar or minister. He or she gets prayed for a lot along with the assistant minister or curate, so they must be important. Then there are overseas missionaries. We show regular concern for them too. Then there are elders and deacons. We don't really know what the difference is between those two, but it's probably something to do with status and promotion. Then there are the home missionaries. We aren't quite sure what they do, because they aren't in Africa like proper missionaries, but we are sure they are very worthy anyway. Then there are home-group leaders, Sunday-school teachers, the verger and people who help in the office and crèche, well-respected Christians in the secular workplace and finally everyone else at the bottom of the sump.

Measuring successful Christian living?

If we let ourselves be persuaded that the way the world measures success translates into Christian living, then the quantity of our activity, or our public face in the church, can become the measure of our Christian life. We can use measures such as whether we have led anyone to the Lord recently, or whether we lead a home group. Leaders can judge themselves according to how many sermons they have preached or Sunday-school classes they have led. In short, we can evaluate our Christianity by whether we think we have performed adequately. Have we lived up to our church's expectations of us, or have we disappointed them? Can we validate our Christian life to our conscience because we think we have done enough?

This is a particular problem for many ministers and church workers. Very often the pressures and expectations on them are high and there are no fixed hours of work. Therefore, because the needs in their churches are great, ministers often see no alternative to working to the point of burnout. And it's not just ministers who can do this. Many Christians find it easy to play the comparisons game, to feel substandard because someone else is being more obviously fruitful or busy, and then try to rectify the problem by working harder. We can all be in danger of importing worldly target-setting into our Christian lives. When we do, there is the possibility that we place ourselves not under the authority of the Lord, but under the expectations of others. We try to please them, rather than him, by our outward conformity to their expectations (or what we think they expect).

The problem with measuring our Christian life by our activity is that it doesn't work. Outward work motivated by a performance mentality is not the same as Christian growth, no matter how much impressive activity it leads to. Worse still, when we buy into this understanding of growth we start to aim at the wrong things – things that *inhibit* Christian growth, such as pursuing praise from other people. Of course, our joy evaporates because we are now *driven* by presentation and show, rather than being *drawn* by grace.

Should I pay God back for grace?

The most subtle version of the problem is usually stated in terms of 'God has done so much for me, so now I have to return the favour by doing a great deal for him.' It sounds holy when we say this, because it is right to want to do good works. However, we must never do them as a payback for receiving grace. For to try to pay back for grace stops it *being* grace, and turns it into something we think God needs remuneration for: 'God gives me grace; I must find something to give in return.' Paul warned against thinking that we can work to pay God back:

> Now when a man works, his wages are not credited to him as a gift, but as an obligation. However, to the man who does not work but trusts God who justifies the wicked, his faith is credited as righteousness.
> (Romans 4:4)

Of course, this is not saying that Christians should never serve or do any good deeds. It is saying that if we insist on working off grace, then we are treating it like a wage that God is obliged to give us. But a gift is not a wage and it is wrong to think we must work to pay back for it.

According to Paul, the thing that justifies wicked people (everyone) is not working for salvation, but trusting God and putting faith in him. If we think we have to pay back, then we are not trusting him alone and don't have faith, and the thing we want to achieve by working slips away from us because it is *only* available by faith. To think we can or should pay back for grace is like receiving a birthday present and asking, 'How much did it cost? Can I pay you back for it?' It is an insult to God's generosity to say, 'You have been gracious to me, but I would rather pay you than receive freely from you.'

Do Christians grow through religion?

Similar issues faced the churches that the apostle Paul had founded in Galatia. People started to teach that God needed paying back. Their teaching had a particular religious (and therefore plausible-sounding) twist to it. The twist was that it was fine to *become* a Christian through receiving grace, but henceforward *continuing* as a Christian depended on obeying the rules and regulations set down for God's Old Testament people, the Jews. You can read all about these rules and regulations of the Old Covenant (collectively called the law of Moses) in the books of Exodus, Leviticus, Numbers and Deuteronomy. The false teachers in Galatia were saying that fullness of Christian living comes from obeying the law of Moses. It must have sounded pretty holy. Maybe their case went something like this.

'It is great that you Gentiles have now become Christians, following the Messiah Jesus. But Jesus was a Jew, and God has given the Jewish people all sorts of rules to follow in order to live a holy life and to please him. Jesus always kept the rules, and so must we if we want to follow him properly. Yes, you are *saved* by trusting Jesus, but you grow in holiness by obeying the law of Moses. The law is how you can know what it means to be godly and holy.'

This sounds very persuasive. Lots of Christians have heard similar things taught in churches from the time we were in Sunday school. If we hear somebody actually say 'You have to do good things in order to please God,' our biblical antennae might tell us something is wrong, but if it is couched slightly differently it can be harder to spot the error. For example:

1. The whole Bible is God's Word.
2. God's Old Testament people were clearly commanded to obey the law.
3. The New Testament says that the law is holy and that the Old Testament commandment is holy, righteous and good (Romans 7:12).
4. Jesus himself said that he hadn't come to abolish the law and that the law will never pass away (Matthew 5:17–18).
5. Christians now have the Holy Spirit who helps and equips us to obey the law.

I recently heard a children's song written to help memorization of the Ten Commandments. The song says that we cannot obey them until we come to Jesus, but concludes with the line that Christians can 'now by love the law obey'. It all sounds logical and biblical and we can see how teachers in Galatia might easily make a case that Christian living depends on obeying the law. By this understanding the purpose and goal of the Holy Spirit living in believers is to empower us to obey the Old Testament law.

But the above argument is wrong and the logic is flawed. The whole of the letter to the Galatians is written to refute it and to introduce correct teaching about how Christians relate to the law. Paul contrasts Old Covenant religion with real Christ-saturated, joy-filled, cross-centred Christianity to lead to the conclusion that 'God has ordained that the goal of the law be fulfilled in us through Christ-loving, not law-keeping'.[1]

Don't desert the gospel of grace

Here are the main headlines of Paul's teaching in Galatians. It is not the easiest book in the New Testament, but full of soul-satisfying truth. I urge you to read it slowly and repeatedly.

Paul is very quick to tell the Galatians that they are straying from the true good news of Jesus. Many of his other letters start with warm greetings and prayers, but Galatians begins with a startling rebuke:

> I am astonished that you are so quickly deserting the one who called you by the grace of Christ and are turning to a different gospel – which is really no gospel at all. Evidently some people are throwing you into confusion and are trying to pervert the gospel of Christ ... As we have already said, so now I say again: If anybody is preaching to you a gospel other than what you accepted, let him be eternally condemned!
> (Galatians 1:6–7, 9)

This is strong stuff! Paul is *really* concerned for the churches in Galatia. They are receiving false teaching, actually another gospel, which is extremely serious. They were leaving behind the apostolic teaching about Christ in favour of something that looked more spiritual or sophisticated, but which was potentially fatal to their faith. In drifting away from the apostle's teaching they were also drifting away from Christ and from his grace, lured by attractive-sounding teaching. There can be teaching that looks holy, but in fact perverts the gospel of Christ. Christians always need to be very careful and discerning about everything we hear from speakers and read in books (even this one!), making sure it is actually what the Bible teaches.

The false teaching doing the rounds in Galatia was that Christians grow by obeying the law of Moses and performing the rituals and expectations of Old Testament religion. Paul makes it clear that all Christians know we are justified by grace, through faith:

> We who are Jews by birth and not 'Gentile sinners' know that a man is not justified by observing the law, but by faith in Jesus Christ . . . by observing the law no-one will be justified.
> (Galatians 2:15–16)

But he also makes it clear that the way Christians grow and are sanctified (made progressively more holy) is *not* by obeying the law:

> You foolish Galatians! Who has bewitched you? Before your very eyes Jesus Christ was clearly portrayed as crucified. I would like to learn just one thing from you: Did you receive the Spirit by observing the law, or by believing what you heard? Are you so foolish? After beginning with the Spirit, are you now trying to attain your goal by human effort? Have you suffered so much for nothing – if it really was for nothing? Does God give you his Spirit and work miracles among you because you observe the law, or because you believe what you heard?
> (Galatians 3:1–5)

They did not receive the Spirit by obeying the law but by believing the gospel. God did not give his Spirit and work miracles among them because they observed the law but because they believed God. Paul sums up that they *became* Christians by faith and they must *grow* as Christians by faith: 'After *beginning* with the Spirit, are you *now* trying to obtain your goal by human effort?'

They had started so well, trusting Jesus to save them and to make them holy. They knew the work of the Holy Spirit doing this in them. But now they were being persuaded that this wasn't enough and that they also needed to obey the Old Testament law to continue in these things. That is, to replace the work of the Holy Spirit (which God does in Christians through faith in Jesus) with human effort to make ourselves acceptable to God. It is another gospel. In Galatians 5 Paul says this is like trying to *justify ourselves*, and that anyone who tries to do it has fallen away from grace and has been alienated from Christ.

We mustn't live our Christian lives measuring our performance of good works to try to tell whether we are good enough for God. It doesn't work; it alienates us from Christ and encourages us to forget about grace and trust ourselves. It is lethal, containing no assurance (because we can never be good enough) and nothing of the Holy Spirit.

Paul continues:

> The law is not based on faith ... Christ redeemed us from the curse of the law by becoming a curse for us ... He redeemed us in order that the blessing given to Abraham might come to the Gentiles through Christ Jesus, so that by faith we might receive the promise of the Spirit.
>
> (Galatians 3:12–14)

Christ has made all the blessings of God available for believers! He has redeemed and given the Holy Spirit to those who have faith in him. The law can't do it. Performance of religion can't do it. Lists of rules for moral behaviour can't do it. We can't do it for ourselves. We can trust only Jesus. To put confidence in anything else is effectively to be enslaved (Galatians 5:1). Trying to be a Christian by the law is like the Greek myth of Sisyphus, who was condemned to the never-ending task of pushing a boulder up a mountain, only to have it roll straight back down to the bottom, where he had to start again. It is futile.

What happens if we forsake grace for law?

You may be wondering if this is really all that important or whether it is just a theological debating point. It *is* important. It is vital enough to have a whole book of the Bible about it. The major importance for you and me is in four areas.

1. Grace is the real gospel

It is the real gospel. If we don't believe it, we don't have the real good news. Instead we have religion masquerading as good news, but that really keeps us enslaved. The real gospel is the gospel of God's grace to us in Jesus. If we don't trust his grace, we will trust something else, whether it is the Old Testament law or little Christian laws of performance we make for ourselves: *Don't go there; don't touch that; don't talk to that person*. It is perilously easy to fall into mere religion or religious culture. We may mistake it for authentic Christian behaviour because it seems to look externally holy.

You may well ask whether holiness is important now we are under grace not law. The answer is 'YES!' It is terrifically important, but obeying the law is not the way to grow in it. We will look more closely at this question in chapters 4 and 9. You may immediately think of verses that clearly command Christians to work out our salvation (e.g. Colossians 3:5–10; Ephesians 4:17 – 5:20; James 1:22ff.; and many other passages in the epistles). In chapter 9 we will see that submission to the Holy Spirit rather than obeying the law produces righteous fruit and growth in holiness. Living under grace rather than law does not lower the bar on holy living (the standard is still there), but it is the Holy Spirit who sanctifies us, rather than our feeble attempts to obey the law.

2. Grace is critical for joy

It is vital to grasp that Christians are under grace, not law, because it is critical for our joy in the Lord. Paul exasperatedly asks the Galatians where all their joy has gone (4:15). They used to have joy in God. They also used to have joy in Paul, who had brought them the good news. Now it seems they don't have either. They are drifting from the good news and from fellowship with the person who brought them the good news.

It is easy to see why. When we know there is nothing we can do to help ourselves or save ourselves, nothing in ourselves to make us holy, then we receive God's grace with complete and utter joy and amazement. We know it is what we have been looking and yearning for. We know it is what the world needs to hear, the answer to being fallen sinful people who can never be good enough. We discover that God gives us Jesus and, along with him, every spiritual blessing – just because he wants to, so people will see his splendid nature and worship him.

When we forget about grace, we set ourselves the impossible task of being good enough. Rather than receiving all we need to live the Christian life from God, we try to work it up from inside ourselves by our dutiful, but unsatisfactory, performance. There is nothing worse than having perpetually to perform a task we cannot achieve (and know we cannot achieve). It very quickly becomes dry and spiritually stale. Perhaps we keep on doing the activity and living the show because others expect it of us, but we end up with a huge gulf between the outside show we put on, with all its 'Christianized' expectations, and the paucity of our hearts, which are dying within us for lack of the living water of grace. And therein lies the lack of joy in Galatia. They were being told that they *had* to do something that can't be done – namely, obey the law of Moses. That is the heart of legalism.

I once met a student group called 'The Doctrine Society' at a university. They were very strong on teaching. They really wanted to pray. And they clearly and overtly taught everyone who came to the group that unless they diligently obeyed the whole of the Old Testament law, then they were disobedient Christians. They left lots of casualties in their wake, because they taught a wrong gospel.

Before you think that is an extreme example, ask yourself about the teaching you receive in church, or your children receive in Sunday school. I think Sunday-school teachers do a brilliant job, against huge odds, and am so glad that they have a gift for it that I badly lack! One thing I recall from my own days in Sunday school was how much we liked to hear Old Testament stories. There is plenty of colour to brighten any Sunday-school lesson in stories like David and Goliath, the crossing of the Red Sea, or Joseph being sold into slavery. Kids of all ages like stories.

It only takes the slightest nudge, however, to tip over from teaching how the stories point to the need for Jesus, into teaching the whole Old Testament as normative for New Testament believers, even though we know that the Old Testament has been fulfilled by Jesus. Perhaps the most obvious example of this is to teach the giving of the Ten Commandments at Sinai as if it was Christians gathered round the mountain receiving them, not Jews. It's a great story with lots of drama.

Recently I saw a Sunday-school sheet that instructed the children that one of the pictures on the page showed all the people obeying God's Old Testament rules. They were told to colour in the picture that showed obedience and do their best that week to obey the rules too. I shuddered! It was well meant. It tried to introduce the Old

Testament to kids, which is a great thing to do. But it taught the children that authentic Christianity is living by the law and doing their best to obey it. The sheet was pure Old Testament religion, with nothing about Christ or about grace, taught without explanation to kids who would lap it up and let it form their understanding of what it means to be a Christian.

I spend a lot of time working with students. I frequently meet those from Christian homes who, when they are away from home, give up on church and meeting with other Christians. One of the most common reasons is that they associate Christianity not with the wonderful grace of Christ, but with a culture of rules and services, obligations and external conformity. They know often that the external show they put on with their families has no internal reality in their hearts and lives, so they take the first opportunity they can to act with their feet. I can't really blame them. On the occasions when I chat to them I often find that their understanding of Christianity is 'Christian subculture' rather than the real thing. There is no joy in mere Christian culture, no delight in salvation. The heart doesn't pump fast when contemplating how to live up to the expectations of Christians rather than genuinely knowing the Lord.

3. Grace stops us being people-pleasers

It is vital to grasp hold of grace, because if we don't, we will let other people, rather than the gospel, dictate our behaviour. We in turn will apply our cultural expectations of Christian behaviour to others. A colleague of mine likes to ask, 'When I am with Christians from different church backgrounds, do I want to act like them (e.g. in worship) because it is godly and helpful to act like them, or because I want to be liked by them?' The first is good, reflecting Paul's desire not to put hurdles in the way of Christians' growth (1 Corinthians 9:19ff.), but the second places him under the authority of people's expectations rather than the authority of the Lord.

There is a striking example of this in Galatians 2:11–14. The apostle Peter was staying with newly converted Gentiles in Antioch. He knew that Old Testament religious observances such as food laws and other matters of ritual purity were no longer relevant to him as a Christian. He freely ate with Gentiles, which would have been unthinkable to a Jew. Peter had no problem with it at all until some men arrived, claiming to come from James, the leader of the church in Jerusalem, which was composed mainly of converted Jews. Paul writes:

> But when they arrived, he began to draw back and separate himself from the Gentiles because he was afraid of those who belonged to the circumcision group. The other Jews joined him in his hypocrisy, so that by their hypocrisy even Barnabas was led astray.
> (Galatians 2:12–13)

Why should Paul get so upset about who Peter wanted to eat with? Peter let his behaviour be determined in a very public way by something that was contrary to the gospel. Not eating with the Gentiles showed an attitude of deference to those who were advocating Old Testament religion. This 'circumcision group' were teaching that Christianity was not the real deal unless it included teaching Gentiles to obey the law of Moses. Even Peter, the great apostle, could be afraid of what other people thought of him. He tried subtly to change his behaviour to get on the right side of this legalistic group.

We can all descend to being people-pleasers. That is what was happening here. But in the process Peter undermined the good news of grace and modelled to others that they should follow the requirements of the law. First, he allowed the circumcision group to influence him, then his example influenced others, until finally the pressure to conform to the old religious ways was so great that even the most reliable Christians caved in.

It was much more than a matter of Peter's choice of dinner companions. When Paul stepped in, he highlighted the real issue underlying Peter's change in behaviour:

> When I saw that they were not acting in line with the truth of the gospel, I said to Peter in front of them all, 'You are a Jew, yet you live like a Gentile and not like a Jew. How is it, then, that you force Gentiles to follow Jewish customs?'
> (Galatians 2:14)

By changing his behaviour to act in line with law rather than grace Peter was casting doubt on whether the gospel was really about grace alone. He inadvertently misled people from fear of what the circumcision bunch would think of him. If a disciple as reliable as Barnabas was led astray, the issue was clearly serious enough to merit a public rebuke. The wrong teaching had affected the whole group, so the whole group needed to see it being dealt with and put right.

The lesson is to live by grace, to resist attempts by our culture or peers to impose law on our behaviour, and to model grace, not law, to others. If we don't, we can end up placing our subcultural norms or the strong expectations of other people above the grace of the Lord. And that, says Paul, is hypocrisy.

4. Neglecting grace saps power from the Christian life

If we neglect grace in favour of law, we will not live by the Spirit, who is the only power for living the Christian life. There is no victory over sin, and no steps forward in holiness, through obeying the law. There may be a visible outward veneer of doing and saying the 'right' things, but Paul is adamant that having a veneer isn't worth anything. He addresses similar issues in his letter to the church in Philippi where he says that as far as an outward veneer of holiness goes, he had it all while he was a zealous persecutor of the church before he was converted:

> If anyone else thinks he has reasons to put confidence in the flesh,
> I have more: circumcised on the eighth day, of the people of Israel,
> of the tribe of Benjamin, a Hebrew of Hebrews; in regard to the law,
> a Pharisee; as for zeal, persecuting the church; as for legalistic
> righteousness, faultless.
> (Philippians 3:4–6)

It is quite a catalogue of success. Paul perfectly performed everything to do with the law. Anything to do with an outward display of being zealously religious and acceptable he did without fault. He was right there with the in-crowd. But then he writes something really shocking:

> But whatever was to my profit I now consider loss for the sake of
> Christ. What is more, I consider everything a loss compared to the

surpassing greatness of knowing Christ Jesus my Lord, for whose sake I
have lost all things. I consider them rubbish, that I may gain Christ and
be found in him, not having a righteousness of my own that comes
from the law, but that which is through faith in Christ – the
righteousness that comes from God and is by faith.

(Philippians 3:7–9)

Everything that he had previously banked his hopes on, Paul now
considered to be worse than useless. It was not just neutral; it was
positively harmful, because it was a distraction from the place where
real righteousness is found – only in Jesus. All the legalistic religion
that looked good had to go, all his previous confidence was pointless
and misleading. He now considered it to be junk. He says, 'I cannot
have that legal religion *and* Jesus, so I will eject all of the religion and
have Jesus instead, because having Jesus is better. Jesus means that I
don't have to make myself good enough and try for a righteousness
that comes from myself, by obeying the law. Instead I will trust Jesus
and he will give me God's righteousness, which is what I actually
need.'

We can have *either* the law and Old Testament religion, *or* we can
have Christ. But we cannot have both. Trying to have righteousness
by good works and religion is opposed to Jesus because it makes us
trust ourselves. When we do so, we know nothing of the work of the
Holy Spirit in our lives, because the law brings only slavery rather
than the freedom of children of God that comes from the Spirit
(Galatians 4:1–7; Romans 8:15–17).

Let us finish this chapter with some words from Galatians that
highlight the contrast between living by grace and putting ourselves
under law:

Mark my words! I, Paul, tell you that if you let yourselves be
circumcised, Christ will be of no value to you at all. Again I declare
to every man who lets himself be circumcised that he is required to
obey the whole law. You who are trying to be justified by law have
been alienated from Christ; you have fallen away from grace. But by
faith we eagerly await through the Spirit the righteousness for which
we hope.

(Galatians 5:2–5)

Questions

1. Are you ever tempted to trust lists of rules or outward Christian activity as a measure of how well you are doing as a Christian? Why?
2. Are you aware of particular expectations of what makes a good Christian that come from church culture rather than Scripture?
3. Fill in the gaps in these verses from Galatians 3:23–25:

> Before _____ came, we were _____
> by the law, locked up until _____.
> So the law was put in charge to _____ that
> we might be _____. Now that faith
> has come, we are no longer _____
> of the law.

Memorize the verse and pray it through to God with thankfulness.

Notes

1 J. Piper, published sermon on Romans 7. See 'Dead to the Law, Serving in the Spirit 4', <http://www.desiringgod.org/library/sermons/01/022501.html>, accessed 21 July 2004. This quote is taken from a sermon on Romans, but the point applies equally well to the closely related passages in Galatians.

3 From slavery to freedom

Legalism stinks! Trusting anything other than Christ to save us or to sanctify us is rubbish. That is the apostle Paul's conclusion in Philippians 3, as we saw at the end of the last chapter. It must have been a very tough conclusion for him. Before he became a Christian his works and his law-keeping consumed his entire life – his time, energy, passions, heart and mind. To realize that it had all been worthless and in contradiction to the good news of Jesus must have been mind-blowing. It is no wonder he was so opposed to legalism when it started to seep into the churches in Galatia. He knew from personal experience how poisonous it was. When the first whiff of it reached his nostrils, he knew there was a danger that people would start trusting works of law rather than Jesus, just as he had done for so many years.

The letter to the Galatians is a powerful antidote to a false gospel based on works. It shows this 'gospel' up for what it is. It is possible that what you have already read of the message of Galatians has made you uncomfortable with some of your own experience of Christian culture. Wherever we see behaviour, however good, being imposed on believers as a core gospel requirement, when the Bible doesn't, we are looking at legalism.

It can have many manifestations. When we dictate what is an acceptable instrument to play for worship in church and what isn't, and baptize our preferences by making them out to be biblical, that is legalism. When we require a dress code in church, and insist that Scripture agrees with us, that is performance-based legalism too. When we insist that all believers must speak in tongues or raise their hands (or *not* raise their hands and *not* speak in tongues!) we stand on the brink of legalism. When we maintain that New Testament believers must fulfil Old Testament law requirements, without considering how Jesus has fulfilled them, that is definitely legalism.

It is easy to do. We can even turn really good things into legalistic burdens. Take 'quiet times', for example. The idea of spending a portion of every day reading the Bible and praying has been a great help to Christians for generations. It is a very good thing to do. However, as soon as we imply that we *must* do it for our holiness, we have turned a great means of blessing into a contemporary equivalent of a work of the law. What was previously a means of grace and blessing and meeting with God has now become a requirement that must be fulfilled for us to have a subjective sense of being a good Christian, or for us to live up to other people's expectations.

A big gulp moment

I used to give spiritual support and guidance to a small group of students at a particular university Christian Union. They were witnessing on a challenging campus. I worked with the leaders to put together the ultimate programme of speakers and outreach. Good though our programme was, I started to get the feeling that people liked the programme and the teaching more than they loved the Lord. I enjoyed the fact that people liked the programme and it gave me a great sense of achievement. However, the longer we went on, the more I felt something was wrong. I couldn't put my finger on what it was, but I noticed that while the group loved having training sessions on how to do evangelism, they didn't actually do very much of it. When they did, it was with reluctance and hesitation. They knew *how*, but they didn't *want* to.

Finally I was asked to do my umpteenth talk on evangelism for them. I began by asking, 'We all know each other well, and so would appreciate an honest answer to this question: When you do evangelism, why do you do it?'

There was a lengthy pause. At last the group said unanimously, 'Because you make us feel guilty when we don't. We feel like we let you down. We do it occasionally out of good form and because we know we should, but that's about it.'

It was one of those big gulp moments in my life. All of a sudden God put his finger on the spot and made me realize that for two years I had produced a programme that *looked* fantastic but was completely disconnected from what was going on in the hearts of the students. Or more exactly, what *wasn't* going on in their hearts. I had tried to make them conform to my expectations, but had neglected nurturing their souls. There was no grace in that situation, only legalism. And, of course, on the few occasions when they did share about the gospel, it was likely to seem insincere or unappetizing to non-believers, because it was coming from grudging obligation rather than hearts saturated with grace and joy.

Grace is the foundation

Evangelism is a great thing to do. But an evangelistic programme done grudgingly without grace is a terrible thing. My experience with that group set me thinking. In my work I have often had the chance to teach people about evangelism, prayer, how to preach, small-group leadership and a host of other things to do with producing an effective, witnessing Christian Union or church. But over a period I came to realize that knowing and experiencing the grace of the Lord is the bedrock of absolutely everything else in the Christian life and in the church. It is the heart of the gospel.

Why should that group have been motivated to do enthusiastic and heartfelt outreach if they were not thrilled and gripped by the grace of the Lord? Why should Christians want to pray to God unless we are convinced that he graciously wants to answer and pour out blessings that will help us and glorify himself? Is it possible to be an effective Christian teacher or preacher unless we are awestruck by the magnitude of grace dealing with our sin, inadequacy and bankruptcy? I doubt it. Preachers who preach without an overwhelming knowledge of grace in their lives don't proclaim grace to their people. They are more likely to teach moral behaviour and how to be an acceptable part of the Christian subculture.

Praying is good, evangelism is good, quiet times and many other Christian disciplines are good. But they are good because they are means of grace and of God being glorified. Grace is the empowering engine behind all of them. When our hearts overflow with the knowledge of his goodness to us and the experience of his favour, then we do all those things and many more, expecting to know more grace as we step out in his service. Without a grace motivation Christian service eventually tires out because we are labouring in our own strength and not in the strength of the Lord. There is no reason to live out the Christian life unless grace is our regular experience and delight. No reason to serve, pray, witness, teach or preach.

The Christian life is a little like a balloon. It is inflated by what God is doing in our hearts, through the Holy Spirit. When there is no breath inflating the balloon, its shape and span are unsustainable. Eventually it deflates and goes limp. This is the contrast between living under grace and living by law. To stretch the illustration a bit, receiving grace pumps up the balloon of Christian living so that it is effective, whereas law merely tells us what an inflated balloon should look like, but doesn't pump it up. In law there is no power over sin, no power for righteous living or for change and growth. All of that comes exclusively from grace.

Are you living as a slave or a son?

You may have read this far and found yourself resonating with the need to receive grace, which is at the heart of Paul's letter to the Galatians. You may be active in Christian service, determined to live out a moral life, but know secretly inside that it is a matter of you driving yourself to it. You might know what it is like to feel deflated in the Christian life, but be unable to admit it for fear of what others might think. You might be in the position of a friend of mine who said, 'I don't think I have ever known anything like what the Bible describes as Christian joy – not from when I was converted until now.' You might be in a church where the grace of the Lord is never talked about or preached on, or where you are never encouraged to reckon on it and make it your own. It may be that you are never with other Christians for whom normal conversation includes delighting in what the Lord is doing in life, conversation that would help you remember about grace and be thankful for it every day.

The apostle Paul describes trying to live the Christian life under law as 'slavery'. We might call it 'churchianity', or 'performance-mentality-for-righteousness'. You may know what that feels like: always having to try to prove yourself to show you are as spiritual as everyone else. There are many vulnerable Christians who never dare demonstrate their vulnerability to anyone in their church, lest everyone else pretends the vulnerable one is the only Christian who ever has any problems with sin or temptation or doubt. Whenever that happens, that place is a haven for legalism, for slavery, for being desperate to be seen to have the right outward religion. It is likely to be a desert of grace.

Escaping the desert of grace

Is there an alternative? What is the answer to living in a desert of grace? It won't surprise you to know that Paul has a lot to say about that in Galatians.

Answer 1: Know your identity in Christ
The first thing Paul wants the believers in Galatia to grasp is who they are in Jesus. They are not slaves to the law. Instead they are sons of God because they belong to Christ (remember from chapter 1 that the use of 'son' may sound sexist, but it isn't because it is the Bible's language for being an heir).

> You are all sons of God through faith in Christ Jesus, for all of you who were baptised into Christ have clothed yourselves with Christ ... If you belong to Christ, then you are Abraham's seed and heirs according to the promise.
>
> What I am saying is that as long as the heir is a child, he is no different from a slave, although he owns the whole estate ... So also, when we were children, we were in slavery under the basic principles of the world. But when the time had fully come, God sent his Son, born of a woman, born under law, to redeem those under law, that we might receive the full rights of sons. Because you are sons, God sent the Spirit of his Son into our hearts, the Spirit who calls out, 'Abba, Father.'

So you are no longer a slave, but a son; and since you are a son, God
has made you also an heir.
(Galatians 3:26 – 4:7)

These verses speak volumes about the identity of Christians. Christians are heirs of God's promises of blessing to Abraham. We are sons
of God, not slaves of the law. We are redeemed. God has sent his Holy
Spirit into our hearts and he makes us want to cry out, 'Abba, Father!',
words that display an amazing family closeness, which supersedes
anything this world has to offer. Christians are 'clothed' with Christ –
literally having his righteousness 'put on us like a coat', in the place of
our own righteousness that was like living in filthy, squalid rags.

If you are a Christian, this is who you *are*. You might not feel like
it, but it is true. If you have trusted Jesus to save you, but haven't
heard about these things before, you should pray now and thank God
for each of them. It may be that over a period you need to pray that
God will bring your feelings into line with the reality – that you are a
royal child of the King! This is the first antidote to living in a desert
of grace. Discovering the reality of our identity in Christ is like
coming to the edge of the desert and finding a pool of cool, refreshing
water to drink and then throwing ourselves into it! This is what God
says about us! Enjoy it with thankfulness and praise.

Answer 2: Live out your identity in Christ
The second answer to living in the grace-desert is to decide that we are
not going to live as slaves. Imagine two young men of similar age in
the ancient Roman world. They might look similar, they might live
and work in the same house. But if one is the son of the house and one
is a slave, the difference between them could not be greater. One is
loved; the other is owned. One has rights and privileges; the other has
none. One will inherit his father's estate; the other has no claim.

Galatians 4:21–31 explains that Christians are not like the slave who
receives none of God's promises, but are free sons who receive all his
promises in Jesus. The illustration finishes by saying:

But what does the Scripture say? 'Get rid of the slave woman and her
son, for the slave woman's son will never share in the inheritance with
the free woman's son.' Therefore, brothers, we are not children of the

slave woman, but of the free woman. It is for freedom that Christ has
set us free. Stand firm, then, and do not let yourselves be burdened
again by a yoke of slavery.
(Galatians 4:30 – 5:1)

The slave woman and her son represent living under the law,
receiving none of God's grace nor the inheritance. The free woman
and her son represent those who are under grace, who receive all of
God's promises. Legalism and grace are as mutually exclusive as
slavery and freedom, which means it is not possible to trust Jesus *and*
wish to live under the law, because those under law are excluded
from the promise.

But that is what the false teachers were telling the Christians in
Galatia: it was great to have Jesus, but they must have the law as well.
Paul says that if we ever hear or see anything like that, we are to stand
firm and have nothing to do with it. We need to decide firmly that we
are going to live free, because it was for the very sake of freedom
from the law that Jesus died. We must take care not to be burdened
again by the yoke of slavery – the law.

Don't live as a slave! Don't act like a slave. Don't let other people
insist that you should be enslaved under Old Testament religious
observance if you want to be a 'proper' Christian. It is legalism and
opposes the grace of God.

Paul goes on:

Mark my words! I, Paul, tell you that if you let yourselves be
circumcised [a sure sign of being under the law], Christ will be of no
value to you at all.
(Galatians 5:2)

The reason Christ will be of no value to you if you want to be
under law is found in Colossians:

When you were dead in your sins and in the uncircumcision of your
sinful nature, God made you alive with Christ. He forgave us all our sins,
having cancelled the written code, with its regulations, that was against
us and that stood opposed to us; he took it away, nailing it to the cross.
(Colossians 2:13–14)

Jesus died to take away the condemnatory power of the law. God made us alive with Christ. If we wish to be under the law, Christ is of no value – because we show that we do not want to be made alive by the power of the cross.

Resist legalism. Give thanks every day for grace. Ask God for more grace and never set grace aside. Decide that this is how you will think and live and ask for God's help. Believe true and accurate things about yourself.

Answer 3: Eagerly look forward to heaven

The third way to walk out of the grace-desert is to await eagerly what God has promised. Galatians 5:5 says that we eagerly await the righteousness we hope for, through the Holy Spirit. At a first reading this sounds strange. After all, didn't we receive the righteousness of Jesus when we became Christians? How then can Paul say we still look forward to the righteousness for which we hope?

While we are still here on Earth, there will always be a battle with sin. We all know that from our experience and the Bible bears it out. However, being 'in Christ' means that God declares us to be righteous in his sight. It is not that we have stopped sinning, or have yet been given the whole extent of that righteousness, but God counts us as completely righteous because Jesus paid for our sins and took the penalty for them.

This does *not* mean that we are yet totally righteous or sinless. But one day we will be. The Bible says that when Jesus takes us to heaven, we will be fully righteous. We will receive a fullness of grace we don't currently have (cf. 1 Peter 1:13). Sin and death will no longer have anything to do with us. We should live in the present eagerly longing for that fullness and looking forward to it with hope and joy. We know it is coming because we have the Holy Spirit, who helps us wait with faith and certainty.

To summarize, Paul offers three ways to make sure we are living under grace, not law:

- Recognizing who we are, our real identity in Jesus.
- Determining that we will live out who we are, standing firm in grace and not letting ourselves be burdened by the enslaving yoke of the law.

- Eagerly looking forward, with the help of the Holy Spirit, to the hope of righteousness that one day will be fully ours. Like children waiting for Christmas, we know it isn't here yet, but the promise of presents is just as real and just as exciting!

Living in grace

We have already seen in Romans 5 what it means to live in grace:

> For if, by the trespass of the one man [Adam], death reigned through that one man, how much more will those who receive God's abundant provision of grace and of the gift of righteousness reign in life through the one man, Jesus Christ.
>
> (Romans 5:17)

Adam sinned and, as a result, all people experienced death. Jesus obeyed the Father and did not sin, so all who trust him and receive his grace and gift of righteousness reign in life through him. The path to reigning in life is not doing but receiving. We can write down the principle like this:

Living in grace = reigning in life

Galatians adds a third element to this principle. Paul refers to living in grace and reigning in life with the phrase 'living by the Spirit' (5:16). We will think a lot more about living by the Spirit in chapter 9, but I want you to see this equation:

Living in grace = reigning in life = living by the Holy Spirit

Living by the Spirit is real Christian living. It is the opposite of living by the law. It is not difficult to understand what it is or how to do it – it is simply receiving and living in the freedom of God's grace and righteousness.

Yes, but how?

So how do we receive grace? I believe it is easy. There is nothing mystical or superspiritual about it. It is the currency of everyday

Christian living. Here is what a believer will look like who holds out her hands to receive grace.

1. She will be a person who clearly and joyfully believes the good news about Jesus. Galatians says that joy in God is a by-product of living by grace. The person who knows what receiving grace is like cannot do anything but joyfully ask for more. More of God's work in her life, a greater appreciation of the wonder of the gospel, a deeper knowledge of the Holy Spirit convicting of sin and assuring of forgiveness, a deeper desire for God to grow her character and for holy fruitfulness. The person who wants to live by grace but cannot recognize these desires in her heart needs to pray that God will do these things in her in a fresh and new way.

2. She will be someone who eagerly looks for and desires the work of the Holy Spirit in her life. She wants to know the guidance of the Holy Spirit leading her in holiness. She is delighted when he does. Galatians 5:16 says, 'live by the Spirit, and you will not gratify the desires of the sinful nature'. As she walks with the Spirit the desires of her sinful nature will be displaced by the Spirit. It is not a promise of perfection and sinlessness this side of heaven, but it does hold out hope for progress in holiness in this life, not by obeying the law, but by trusting in the help of the Holy Spirit.

3. She will be someone who asks God to take control of her life and make her character like his. Galatians 5:22 says that the fruit God will produce in lives yielded to him is love, joy, peace, patience, kindness, goodness, faithfulness, gentleness and self-control. When we see a person growing in these things and modelling them to all around, we see someone receiving grace. It's good to pray that God will do this in us.

4. She will be a person who counts herself dead to sin and alive to Jesus (5:24). She will be looking for opportunities to love God and be like him, and for ways to avoid being unlike him (by sinning). She delights in God – she is bowled over by him. She wants nothing more than to walk with him and to know him better and better. She doesn't want anything to get in the way of that, so she willingly and knowingly puts other things aside because she thinks that God is better than anything else.

This is walking by the Spirit and receiving grace. It is so different from righteousness by law-keeping. I like to think of it with two diagrams.

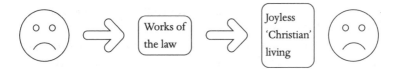

In this first diagram the sinful person on the left wonders how he can ever be good enough for God. He is taught that he needs to perform well and do good works so that God will be pleased. He tries to put this into practice in Christian living. Unfortunately it doesn't work, because law has no power to produce good in us, so he wears a mask of works in order to be seen to measure up, but knows no joy.

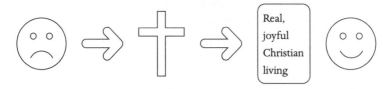

In this second diagram the sinful person wonders how he can be good enough for God and hears that, because of the death of Jesus, God will accept him freely by grace. In his heart he humbles himself, asks God to forgive him because of Jesus and experiences God's grace freely given to him. He goes on to live as a Christian because he expects to receive all the benefits that flow from God's grace, through the cross of Jesus. He knows sure hope and the joy of realizing Jesus has done everything he cannot do for himself.

These two people could well appear quite similar on the outside, like the illustration of the son and the slave. They both start off with an awareness of their sin and both end up exhibiting a form of Christian behaviour. The difference is what happens in the middle – which is invisible to the world because it happens in Christians' hearts – and the consequent outcome in joy or joylessness.

In the first case, trusting religious works does not make the grade, because there is no power for Christian living. In this instance the person tries to do it himself. But eventually a widening gulf opens between the outside 'Christian' face he shows the world and the fact that his heart is shrivelled up and dying inside. In the second case, however, there is no gulf between the heart and the outside, because the Christian is being empowered by receiving God's grace.

The two cases may look similar but could not be more different. The second is costly. It means confessing your sin and your need. It means honestly confronting the fact that you can never be good enough for God and admitting you are totally dependent on him and his grace. But it is the only way. And it is the joyful way. It is the way into the arms of a loving Father who longs to pour out grace on grace to those who will receive it. It is the antidote to legalism, the necessary remedy for law-based religion mired in failed attempts at making our own righteousness.

If you know you are trying to make yourself good enough, trusting your own righteousness to save you or to make you holy, I plead with you to stop right now and turn to God for grace. You might like to pray a prayer like the one below:

Dear heavenly Father,
I've heard about your grace. I realize that I rarely trust you and ask you for it. Sometimes I try to make myself good enough, but I always fail. I've believed the lie that I should be independent and not rely on help from you. Often I've not desired to walk by the Holy Spirit.

Please forgive me and give me a desire to know your wonderful grace every day. Let me know the work of your Spirit in my life, producing his fruit and helping me walk with you. With your help I want to turn my back on a religion of works and learn to receive your abundant provision of grace and the free gift of righteousness.
Amen

Questions

1. Imagine sharing the good news with a friend motivated not by grace but by fear of what others will think if you don't. What would such evangelism look and feel like?

2. The Bible says that Christians are royal children of God rather than slaves. How do you feel about having this status given to you?

3. One of the ways out of the grace-desert is eagerly to await the righteousness for which we hope. Do you spend much time reflecting on heaven and the return of Jesus Christ? If not, why not?

4 *Really* under grace, not law?

As I have spent time teaching and preaching that Christians are not under law but under grace I have been asked many times whether the law, especially the Ten Commandments, is still a useful guide to moral behaviour. People reason that because the Ten Commandments reveal the character of God, and that Old Testament Israel was commanded to obey the law, obedience to the law is therefore a useful way to holiness for Christians. Others believe that the Ten Commandments provide a useful checklist by which to measure progress in Christian living.

How should we consider these important issues? Many New Testament passages speak about the need for holy behaviour, the importance of working out our salvation once we become Christians, and the crucial need for obedience to God through Jesus Christ. I believe that holiness and obedience to God are absolutely vital in the Christian life. However, in this chapter I will try to show from the Bible that holiness does not come from being under the law and still less from being under contemporary rules for behaviour. The law was not given to produce holiness through obedience to it, but to highlight sinfulness as God's Old Testament people realized they could *never* obey it. The purpose of having a law that couldn't make them holy was to lead them to a saviour who could.

This chapter will help you get to grips with some vital truths. It deals with some tough issues, but stick with it and you will find it worthwhile.[1]

Acts 15: a practical case study on law and grace

Helpful reading: Acts 15:1–21

Acts 15 is a good place to start. In this chapter of the Bible the issue of law and grace is highlighted in the context of local churches while the apostles were present to resolve it. The episode begins with the same incident we have already read about in Galatians 2. Some men who claimed to come from James in Jerusalem (but in fact didn't: see 15:24) went to Antioch and started to teach, 'Unless you are circumcised, according to the custom taught by Moses, you cannot be saved' (verse 1). This led Peter to stop associating with Gentiles and it directed lots of people away from the truth of the gospel, even including Barnabas. This brought Paul and Barnabas into a dispute with the false teachers, which Luke records in Acts 15:2.

Eventually it was decided that Paul and Barnabas, along with some of the other believers, should go to Jerusalem to see the apostles and elders there to settle, once and for all, the matter of whether new Gentile believers should be under the law (15:2–4). They received a warm welcome from the church in Jerusalem and described in detail to them what God had been doing among the Gentiles (15:4).

At this point the critical issue was raised. Verse 5 says that some of the believers who were from the party of the Pharisees stood up and said, 'The Gentiles must be circumcised and required to obey the law of Moses.' There it is, the core issue, right out on the table.

The apostles and elders met to consider the question. It must have been quite a meeting. We are told there was 'much discussion'! Finally Peter put a powerful case with which everyone agreed (including the Holy Spirit, 15:28!). We can follow his case from verse 7. First he reminded the apostles and elders how God had allowed Gentiles to hear the good news from him, and how they believed it and were converted (see Acts 10 and 11). Then he detailed how God had clearly and visibly accepted the Gentiles by giving them the Holy Spirit, just as he had previously given the Spirit to Jewish believers.

The clear way to see that the Gentiles had become Christians was that God had purified their hearts through faith in Jesus, just as it had been with all of them (15:9).

Then came the crunch. 'Now then, why', Peter asked, 'do you try to test God by putting on the necks of the disciples a yoke [the law] that neither we nor our fathers have been able to bear? No! We believe it is through the grace of our Lord Jesus that we are saved, just as they are' (15:10–11).

When they had all listened carefully to everything, James confirmed that the conversion of the Gentiles was exactly what God had promised through the prophets (15:15–18). He then made a concluding judgment that it should not be made difficult for the Gentiles to turn to the Lord by imposing the law on them. Instead they should be required to abstain from food polluted by idols, from sexual immorality, from the meat of strangled animals and from blood.

A new Christian version of the law?

These last four requirements are not the imposition of a new version of the law or some measure of holiness, but rather, as John Calvin helpfully puts it, nothing more 'than what brotherliness calls for'. He says:

> There is an obvious reason for them to make this rule about things offered to idols, blood and animals that have been strangled ... We know that the Lord commands his people to eschew [avoid; abstain from] things that are contrary to the external profession of the faith and in which there is any appearance or suspicion of idolatry. Therefore, lest any taint of superstition should remain in the Gentiles, and lest Jews should see in them anything that did not agree with the pure worship of God, it is not surprising they were commanded to abstain from things offered to idols to avoid giving offence.[2]

John Stott agrees that the issue is how to ensure brotherly fellowship between Jewish believers and the new Gentile Christians:

> Once the theological principle was firmly established, that salvation is by grace alone ... [Paul] was prepared to adjust his practical policies. He made two notable concessions, both for the same conciliatory

reason. First he accepted the four cultural abstentions proposed by Jewish leaders to Gentile converts, because Moses was widely read and preached [Acts 15:21], and this Gentile restraint would ease Jewish consciences and facilitate Jewish–Gentile social intercourse.[3]

Stott's point is well made from the passage. Introducing these abstentions was not a new law. It did not impose some condition for either salvation or sanctification other than grace alone, but merely requested that the new believers behave wisely regarding idols and live helpfully in fellowship with Jewish believers who had tender consciences.

The Acts 15 episode finishes with this being written in a letter to the new Gentile believers. The letter confirmed that they should not be burdened by the law and refuted that the Jerusalem church had sent the teachers of the circumcision group to tell them to obey the law. The Gentile believers received the letter with gladness!

For how long did the law apply?

How then should we respond to the claim that the law continues to be the standard of Christian holiness? After all, didn't Jesus say that the law is permanent (Matthew 5:18)? For this we need to turn to Galatians 3 and Romans 7. Here we discover that the law is indeed permanent, but that Christians are not subject to it. We no longer have any relation to it.

Helpful reading: Galatians 3:6–25

Paul invites the Galatian believers to consider the example of Abraham. Abraham did not try to be right with God by obeying the law. Indeed he couldn't, because the law wasn't given for another 430 years. On the contrary, Abraham was declared righteous by grace, through having faith in God. Verse 6 makes this plain: 'He believed God, and it was credited to him as righteousness.' The Jews thought that they were children of Abraham because they were physically descended from him. Paul, however, claims that Abraham's real children are those who believe in the same way Abraham believed (3:7). This, he says, makes sense of God's promise to Abraham to bless the nations through him (3:8–9).

By contrast, everyone who relies on the law is under the curse of the law, because only someone who can keep it *perfectly* receives the conditional blessings it offered for perfect obedience. Only Jesus ever kept it perfectly. All others who try to be holy by keeping the law find themselves only being cursed by it (3:10–14). Therefore there is no hope for those who look for righteousness in the law. The only hope is found in Christ, who redeemed us from this curse by becoming a curse himself on our behalf (3:13). He redeemed us not so we might subsequently keep the law, but

> in order that the blessing given to Abraham [apart from and before the law] might come to the Gentiles through Christ Jesus, so that by faith we might receive the promise of the Spirit.
> (Galatians 3:14)

In other words we are not saved *to keep the law*; we are saved *from the law*. The law is a curse to sinful people like us, because we can never keep it. It is itself good and right, but when it meets the resistance of sinful hearts, it only ever condemns. We must have Christ to rescue us from it.

Paul continues with an example in 3:15–23 that answers two crucial questions: For how long was the law applicable, and why was the law imposed for that period? The example is about human promises. Paul says, 'If human promises are binding, how much more is God's promise binding?'

> Just as no-one can set aside or add to a human covenant that has been duly established, so it is in this case. The promises were spoken to Abraham and to his seed. The Scripture does not say 'and to seeds', meaning many people, but 'and to your seed', meaning one person, who is Christ. What I mean is this: The law, introduced 430 years later, does not set aside the covenant previously established by God and thus do away with the promise.
> (Galatians 3:15–17)

God gave Abraham a promise that all nations will be blessed through him and his seed, Jesus. Whatever it was the law was introduced to achieve 430 years later, it *could not* be to set aside the promise or make the blessing and inheritance of Abraham dependent on the law instead. For that would mean God broke his promise.

Why was the law given?

By now you can almost hear the outcry from Paul's readers: 'Paul, if the law wasn't given to bring the inheritance, what on earth was it for?' His answer is profound:

> So the law was put in charge to lead us to Christ that we might be justified by faith. Now that faith has come, we are no longer under the supervision of the law.
> (Galatians 3:24)

In other words, the law was introduced by God as a pointer that we need him to send a saviour. And it was put in charge for as long as that need remained, which was until faith was revealed (3:23). Paul fleshes this out further with a very direct question and answer:

> What, then, was the purpose of the law? It was added because of transgressions until the Seed to whom the promise referred had come.
> (Galatians 3:19)

The law was given because of transgressions. It was in operation over believers until the Seed – Jesus – came. Why was it given for transgressions? It was definitely *not* given to impart life (3:21). Instead it held the whole world prisoner to sin, so that the promise might then come to those who believe in Jesus (3:22). Now that Jesus has come, he has completely fulfilled all demands of the law for us, by his life and his work on the cross. This means Christians are no longer subject to the law and no longer slaves, but recipients of the promise and sons of God (4:7). Hallelujah!

Betrothed to Jesus

Helpful reading: Romans 7:1–6

Romans 7 makes the case in a slightly different way. Please pause and read Romans 7:1–6. Here is another example taken from everyday life, this time from marriage. Paul says that the law has authority over people as long as they live: 'Think about it like a marriage,' he says. 'Married people aren't free just to go off and marry other people. That would be unfaithful to their spouse. However, if a spouse dies, then the living person is freed from that marriage and can remarry without being adulterous' (7:2, my paraphrase).

Where death occurs, a person is freed from the law that applies during life. Paul says it is just like this with the Old Testament law of Moses. While we are still alive, it binds us to our sinful nature and we are powerless to do anything about it. However:

> So, my brothers, you also died to the law through the body of Christ, that you might belong to another, to him who was raised from the dead, in order that we might bear fruit to God.
> (Romans 7:4)

When Christ died, everyone in Christ also died with respect to the law. It is not that the *law* died or ceased to exist but that *we* died with respect to it. Verse 6 makes this abundantly clear:

> But now, by dying to what once bound us, we have been released from the law, so that we serve in the new way of the Spirit, and not in the old way of the written code.
> (Romans 7:6)

Paul is adamant that the law is holy, and the commandment is holy, righteous and good (7:12). However, it is also deadly to sinners because we are *not* holy, righteous and good. The good law condemns us as unrighteous, and sin leads us to death. But when we accept Christ's death on our behalf by faith, we are discharged from the law and are now allowed to be betrothed to Jesus.

Terry Virgo has a great illustration about being discharged from the law:

> This release [from the law] is absolutely clear cut and can be likened to a soldier's discharge from the army. Until a certain date the young recruit is subject to all the rigours and disciplines of military training. He is under orders which he is expected to obey to the letter.

But on the day he is discharged he strolls carelessly across the parade ground, a free man. Horrified at the sight of this slovenly soldier, the sergeant bellows out to him the command to return and stand to attention. At first the ex-soldier cringes at the familiar cry. Then he remembers that this man, once his superior, no longer has any authority over him. He raises a hand and waves goodbye. The sergeant can yell for all he is worth, it is of no consequence. He cannot order around someone who has been discharged. The answer to the question, 'are Christians under the law?' is 'No'.[4]

The law was a temporary measure, given 430 years after Abraham, until Christ came. It was given to act as a diagnostic tool, showing the need for a saviour and leading people to Christ. It worked its purpose by highlighting sin, but never solved the problem. It was never intended to – that was not what it was for. A friend of mine explains that, like a thermometer, the law indicated illness but did not cure it.

Does the law still serve any useful purpose for holiness?

My argument will leave many Christians wondering how we can encourage holiness among Christians if the obvious standard of the law is removed, or whether it is possible to teach ethical Christian behaviour without the law to help us know what to do. These are big and sincere questions, with large consequences for how we live as Christians.

We will deal with the theme of holiness in more depth in chapter 9, where we will see that growing in sanctification comes from living by the Spirit. The Bible, Old Testament and New, is full of encouragements, rebukes and commands to obedient, holy and ethical living. Here I want to show briefly that Paul taught that the ethical standard for Christian believers is not the law, but our relationship with Christ.

Romans 6 and 7 are particularly focused on the fact that Christians are under grace, not law (Romans 6:15). Paul's teaching on this subject in Romans has raised some questions for his readers, which he addresses in chapters 6 and 7. Three of these questions are:

- Should we go on sinning so that grace may increase (6:1)?

- Should we sin because we are not under law but under grace (6:15)?
- If the law worked to produce sin in us, does that mean that the law itself is sinful (7:7)?

Answer 1: Be mastered by Christ
Paul teaches that the purpose of the law was to increase transgressions (Romans 5:20). Where sin increased, God wonderfully increased grace to cover it. This is the reason for the first question. If God has given more grace to cover more sin, and grace is a good thing, then why not sin even more, so there is even more grace?

An Old Testament answer to this question would be, 'Don't sin, because the law tells you that you must not.' Paul, however, doesn't go anywhere near that line of reasoning. Instead he offers three reasons not to sin:

- We have died to it in the death of Christ, so we no longer have anything to do with it. We have been crucified with him (6:3, 6). Anyone who has died in this way with Jesus has been freed from sin (6:7).
- We have been raised to new life in Christ that is wholly opposed to sin (6:4).
- Therefore we do not let sin reign, because we have a new master, not sin but Christ (6:14). Previously, under law, sin was the master. But now, under grace, Christ is the master.

This last point is the crucial conclusion. Notice the parallels. Under law we were mastered by sin. Under grace we are mastered by Christ. Is the law the answer when Christians sin? Is the law the place to turn to help us not sin? No! The law is the *old* master. The *new* master, Christ, is where we now turn to find our help. Jesus said that the law and the prophets all pointed prophetically to him. *The New Testament equivalent of obedience to the law is being mastered by Christ.* New Covenant believers don't look to the law to know how to be holy, we look to the gospel.

It is important to note that Paul is *not* saying that Christians no longer sin. Rather he is saying that Christians are no longer *bound* to sin, because we are not under the law. Christian behaviour therefore is not driven by the law, but by counting ourselves dead to sin and alive to God in Christ (6:11). We have been freed to offer our bodies to him as instruments of righteousness, not because the law says so but because we are supernaturally united with Jesus in his death and resurrection (6:5).

Answer 2: Live as a slave of Christ

The second question Paul addresses is a different perspective on the same theme: 'If the standard of the law no longer matters because we are under grace, can we do exactly as we please? Do sin and holiness no longer matter? Shall we sin because we are under grace not law?'

The Old Testament answer would be, 'Don't sin, because the law says so, and you are enslaved to the law.' Once again, however, Paul doesn't pursue that line of reasoning. He is adamant that sin is to be strongly avoided ('By no means!' 6:15), but *not* by obedience to the law. He argues in 6:17 that we used to be slaves of sin but now we have been freed from it by trusting the *gospel* through which we have become slaves to righteousness leading to holiness. This is repeated soon after:

> But now that you have been set free from sin and have become slaves to God, the benefit you reap leads to holiness, and the result is eternal life. For the wages of sin is death, but the gift of God is eternal life in Christ Jesus our Lord.
> (Romans 6:22–23)

Answer 3: Live as the betrothed of Christ

As we have already seen, Paul concludes his argument with the illustration of marriage in 7:1–7. He says that we were once married to the old nature in a covenant that can only be dissolved when one of the partners dies. We were not free just to ditch our old husband and get engaged to Christ. That would be adulterous. However, Christ identifies us so closely with himself in his death that when he died, we also died to the law (7:4). Therefore we can now be engaged again, this time to Jesus. In our new betrothal we are released from the old way of obedience to the written letter (7:6) and are instead enabled to serve in the new way of the Spirit.

Paul makes his case using pairs of opposites:

- marriage to the sinful nature versus betrothal to Christ
- dying to the law versus being made alive to Christ
- bearing fruit for death under the law versus bearing fruit for God through belonging to Christ
- dying to the law that bound versus being released to serve in the Spirit
- being controlled by the sinful nature (the sinful passions being aroused by the law) versus being freed by Christ

So strong are the oppositions that we cannot conclude now, under grace, that we still use the law to make our behaviour holy. That is the exact thing that this passage tells us not to do.

How shall we be holy?
How then *shall* we be holy if not through obeying the law? By trusting Christ! By reckoning on our betrothal to him and relying on the help given by the Holy Spirit. Romans 8 finishes the argument. There is no condemnation from the law for Christians, because by the law of the Spirit of life we are set free from the law of sin and death. The Old Testament law was powerless, but God has done every-thing needed for holiness by sending his Son as a sin offering (8:3). Because of the death of Jesus as our substitute, all the requirements of the law *are* met in us – not by our obeying it, but by Christ's victory over sin.

The answer to the question 'Is holiness important?' is that it is vital, but that teaching law is not the way to guide Christian behaviour or direct ethical standards. The way is to teach the gospel and to encourage believers to reckon on, and live out, our new marriage to Christ.

You might be thinking, 'But that is a lot harder to discern and a lot less clear. How do we know if we are getting it right without the list of standards provided by the law?' Marriages don't usually work by checklists. We get married to a person, not to a set of rules that dictate the mechanisms of successful marriage. My wife does not cook me lovely meals because she took vows to me and is worried about contravening them. She cooks lovely meals out of love for me! The same principle operates with regard to holiness. In our betrothal to Jesus we are not controlled by the rules, but by the Holy Spirit who lives in us. We have our minds set on what the Holy Spirit desires. We look more closely at how this produces holiness in chapter 9.

Holiness and boasting in the cross

At the end of Galatians we discover that the circumcision party (the group who wanted the believers to obey the law) were trying to compel Christians to be circumcised. They were doing this in order to 'avoid being persecuted for the cross of Christ' (Galatians 6:12). It was not that they obeyed the law themselves, but that they wanted the outward form of legalism so that they could boast in their own achievements, not in the cross.

The impact of the cross is that it removes people from being under the law, as they now live by the Spirit. In the Jewish cultural context this was deeply offensive. The circumcision group were trying to avoid being tarred with the offensiveness of the cross of Jesus, and attempted to sidestep the cost of following Christ, by insisting on the requirements of the law.

Paul's case all boils down to the cross. Those who boast in the cross are not under the law: they are under grace; they are walking by the Spirit. Galatians 3 says:

> Before your very eyes Jesus Christ was clearly portrayed as crucified.
> I would like to learn just one thing from you: Did you receive the
> Spirit by observing the law, or by believing what you heard? . . .
> Does God give you his Spirit and work miracles among you because
> you observe the law, or because you believe what you heard?
> (Galatians 3:1–5)

What they had heard and believed was the message of the cross of Jesus. People who consider themselves nothing so that they may boast in the cross, and who believe that Christ was crucified for us, are walking by the Spirit.

How should we teach the Old Testament?

One further question concerns how we should teach the Old Testament, especially passages that are clearly law-based. Many Old

Testament passages delight in God's law. Should we teach them as directly applicable to Christians? And can we teach law evangelistically to non-Christians, using it to highlight sin so that they will repent and ask for grace?

Whole volumes are dedicated to this subject! I hope that as you have followed Paul's argument in Romans and Galatians, you have seen that we should not apply the law directly to Christians. New Covenant believers are not under Old Covenant legislation and practices. The law was summed up, completed, fulfilled and utterly obeyed on our behalf by Christ. We are no longer under it, either for our justification or for our sanctification. People could never obey the condemning law. But it pointed them to the Redeemer, thereby accomplishing its goal. However, we have seen in Romans 6 and 7 that because the goal of the law is accomplished does not lower the bar on holiness or mean that our behaviour no longer matters.

Are we then to ignore and not teach anything from the Old Testament? No! We are to teach the Old Testament in such a way that it points to its own fulfilment in Christ and his glory. It is very easy to approach Old Testament passages with the automatic assumption that anything that God says there about Israel now applies directly to the Christian church, and that everything he says about Jews applies directly to Christians.

These are false assumption for a very important reason: the New Testament equivalent of Old Testament Israel is not directly the church, but the *perfect Israel*, Jesus Christ. The New Testament equivalent of an Old Testament believer is someone who lives in Christ and is filled with the Holy Spirit.

Therefore when we read or teach the Old Testament, we ask not what it tells us directly about *us*, but first what it tells us about *Jesus*. Subsequently we discover, through the lens of Christ, what it teaches about those who are in Christ. In the matter of the law we need to ask first how it applies to Christ (he has perfectly fulfilled it) and only then how it applies to us (we are now under the law of Christ, God's grace, not the Old Testament law).

This is exactly what Jesus teaches on the Emmaus road in Luke 24. He says that the whole of the Old Testament is about him. It is also what Paul teaches in Romans 3:

> But now a righteousness from God, apart from law, has been made
> known, to which the Law and the Prophets testify.
> (Romans 3:21)

Righteousness is not found in the law, but 'apart from law'. Paul
says that the purpose of the law was to be prophetic about Jesus,
pointing to the better way that he has opened up and the better
righteousness he brought. The purpose of the law when the Old
Testament is taught to Christians is to testify to the righteousness of
God found in Jesus.

Perhaps the letter to the Hebrews sums it up best. It was written to
Christian believers who came from a Jewish heritage and aimed
to show that the Old Testament itself always anticipated something
better and more lasting than the Old Covenant, which would make
the Old Covenant obsolete.

Hebrews says that Jesus is the ultimate priest for God's people. He
is not a priest in the Old Testament order, the Levitical priesthood,
but one in a completely different order. It says that when there is such
a change in the priesthood, *there is also a change in the law, for it is given
on the basis of the priesthood*:

> If perfection could have been attained through the Levitical priesthood
> (for on the basis of it the law was given to the people), why was there
> still need for another priest to come – one in the order of Melchizedek,
> not in the order of Aaron? For when there is a change of the priesthood
> there must also be a change of the law.
> (Hebrews 7:11–12)

And then:

> The former regulation is set aside because it was weak and useless
> (for the law made nothing perfect), and a better hope is introduced
> by which we draw near to God.
> (Hebrews 7:18–19)

Hebrews 8 – 10 fills in the detail: Jesus guarantees a better
covenant with better worship, a perfect priesthood, a final sacrifice
and faultless reconciliation with God. All of these things were

foreshadowed in the Old Testament law, but made real and concrete in Jesus:

> The law is only a shadow of the good things that are coming – not the realities themselves.
> (Hebrews 10:1)

We should teach that the law was the shadow of the good news about Jesus, not the good thing itself. It pointed and prophesied in a shadowy way from which we learn about the glory to be revealed later. But now we have the glorious gospel, we do not need the shadow – except to marvel at how it pointed to the Saviour. As the writer to the Hebrews puts it:

> By calling this covenant 'new', he [God] has made the first one obsolete; and what is obsolete and ageing will soon disappear.
> (Hebrews 8:13)

Should we use the law for evangelism?

Is it appropriate, then, to use the law for evangelism? Does it still have a legitimate use in highlighting the sin of non-Christians in order to lead them to Christ? After all, the law did reveal God's character to Old Testament Israel and demanded that they conform to that character. This is another big question with far-reaching implications for our methods of evangelism.

I do not believe evangelism is a legitimate use of law, for two reasons. First it is not a method used in evangelistic settings in the New Testament. In 1 Corinthians 9 Paul clearly says he does not use the law for evangelizing Gentiles:

> Though I am free and belong to no man, I make myself a slave to everyone, to win as many as possible. To the Jews I became like a Jew, to win the Jews. To those under the law I became like one under the law (though I myself am not under the law), so as to win those under the law. To those not having the law I became like one not having the law (though I am not free from God's law but am under Christ's law), so as to win those not having the law.
> (1 Corinthians 9:19–21)

This passage tells us that Paul neither uses the law to convict Gentiles of sin, nor does he consider himself under the law when evangelizing Jews. He sensitively adjusts his cultural approach in order to win people, but maintains throughout that he is not under the law but under 'Christ's law' – that is, grace.

Similarly the law is not used as a method to highlight sin in the evangelistic sermons recorded in Acts. In most of them the charge standing against people is not law-breaking but idolatry, the appeal is based on Jesus and the resurrection, and it is the teaching that Jesus is raised from death as judge that most often brings conviction of sin or denial of the gospel.

The second reason why I do not believe the law should be used in evangelism is because it is wrong to conclude that knowledge of the law is essential before sinners can know they need salvation. Paul contends in Romans 1 that all people know about God plainly and see his eternal power and divine qualities from what has been made. We know enough to seek him and are culpably sinful and without excuse, not for law-breaking, but for suppressing the truth about God that we know and for preferring idols.

Romans 5 then makes the case that sin was in the world before the law. People could be condemned for ignoring God before the law, and could be rescued by trusting the promise before the law. Abraham was saved by faith before the law. It was impossible for him to be convicted of sin or realize that he needed salvation by hearing the law.

Romans 2 therefore says that those who wish to place themselves under the law (Jews) will be condemned by it because they are law-breakers. And those who aren't under it (Gentiles, to whom the law was not given in the first place) will be condemned not by the law but through their consciences, by which they know they are sinners.

Christ has fulfilled the law. He has completed in his cross-work everything the law foreshadowed. We are therefore now in the same position as Abraham and all other people before the law was given. We are condemned for ignoring God, but rescued by the grace of God in order to receive the promise of God. The law is prophetic of Christ and therefore *can* still reveal sin, but is not *essential* for doing so. If we are reading an Old Testament passage that has a clear evangelistic focus as it points to Christ, we should certainly seize the opportunity. But we do not have to import arguments from law into all evangelism.

In the Old Testament the law revealed God's character to Israel in shadow form. In the New Testament Christ perfectly reveals God's character as the exact likeness of his being and the splendour of the Father's glory. The use of the law to convict of sin is therefore unnecessary. It is like relying on the shadow when the reality is present! The seriousness of sin is much more clearly highlighted by people's disobedient rejection of Christ than by their rejection of the shadow of Christ. What they need to hear for conviction is not the law preached but Christ preached. Therefore I conclude that we do not need to teach the law for non-Christians to be convicted of sin by the Holy Spirit and for evangelism to be effective.

Questions

1. Calvin says that abstaining from idol-meat, blood and eating animals that had been strangled was important for expressing 'brotherliness' with other believers. By what principles should we decide what behaviour we need to adopt to encourage Christian fellowship? How can we tell when it turns from brotherliness into law?

2. Why, according to Galatians 3, does the law last only until the Seed of Abraham (Jesus) came?

3. List some of the implications of being 'discharged' from the law.

4. Why is it not legitimate for Christians to sin, even though we are not under law?

Notes

1 For a more detailed recent study on the position I take, see Douglas J. Moo, 'The Law of Christ as Fulfilment of the Law of Moses', in W. Strickland (ed.), *Five Views on Law and Gospel* (Zondervan, 1996), pp. 319–376. This book also helpfully explains views that disagree with my own. Another good introduction to the themes can be found in J. Piper's 2001 sermons on Romans 7 <http://www.desiringgod.org>.

2 John Calvin, *Commentary on Acts*, Crossway Classic Commentaries (Crossway, 1995), p. 264.

3 John Stott, *The Message of Acts*, The Bible Speaks Today (IVP, 1990), p. 256.

4 T. Virgo, *Enjoying the Grace of God* (Kingsway, 1999), p. 25.

Part **2**
Finding joy in radical Christian living

5 Discover a sweeping panorama of joy

Enjoying God – together

Among the Christian students I work with there is a dawning realization that talking about God's grace and celebrating it together is normal Christian living. This and spurring one another on in the Christian life should be the common currency in the church. For many Christians, however, it is tragically rare. Comparatively few Christians in the UK are genuinely concerned for each other's growth and encouragement in the Lord. We find it easy to let the individualistic assumptions of the age slip into our mindset and into our expectations about being the body of Christ together. When two Christians meet, the conversation can often be little or no different from that of two non-Christians. All too often the one who says 'How are things going with God?' or 'What is God doing in your life at the moment?' or even 'Why don't we read a bit of the Bible and pray together?' is considered superspiritual or a bit weird.

I don't know why this should be, but I am convinced that an individualistic attitude is spiritually crippling because it is unbiblical. The vast majority of instructions to churches in the New Testament are written either to groups of Christians about how to live out their faith together, or to individual leaders *about* groups and how to help local churches work out their faith together. When we replace this corporate understanding of discipleship with a lonely and individual one, we remove the single most important thing God has given for encouragement and growth in grace: real fellowship in the body of Christ. There may be many reasons why people distance themselves from the body: suspicion, inferiority or superiority complexes, wanting to hide their sin, hating the idea of dependence, wanting to 'go to church' but to avoid being part of the church. The result in all cases is damage to the body of Christ and its worship and witness.

Growing as a Christian is always corporate. It is never individualistic or selfish. Bearing each other's burdens and reminding each other about the Lord doesn't happen when Christians are isolated. Whatever hurdles we find to genuine fellowship, we must commit ourselves to overcoming them. It may mean summoning up the courage to ask a few other believers if we could meet together to encourage one another in prayer. It may mean that we need to ask if some core teaching on grace can be included in our church's preaching schedule. In the most extreme cases, where there is no likelihood of revitalizing a church, discovering fellowship or growing in grace, it may be necessary to leave and find another church where these things are experienced and rejoiced in.

Priorities for joy

Part 1 of this book dealt with the question 'If someone has no Christian joy, are they living in grace?' In Part 2 we will consider another, related, question: 'If we *have* received grace, then what things does the Bible tell us we should glory and take joy in? What should excite and thrill us? Where do joyful Christians direct their energies and their obedience? In short, what should be our priorities for joy?

I love Paul's letter to the church in Philippi. It is written *from* distressing circumstances (Paul was in prison) *to* distressing circumstances (people in Philippi were preaching with bad motives, fights were breaking out in the church and some members of the circumcision party were starting to teach circumcision and obedience to the law as a further requirement to receiving Christ). The letter is a hearty dose of reality that almost any church or anyone who has been a Christian for a while can relate to. Hardship, bickering, sour relationships and questions about the content of teaching are all quite contemporary, and we find them all in Philippians. However, regardless of the difficulties in Philippi, the letter is bursting with joy. Paul exhorts them to take joy in the Lord. He even commands it, giving reason after reason. He tells them to give expression to their joy, to manifest their enjoyment of God outwardly.

So Philippians is a great book to look at in these next chapters to see a wide-ranging panorama of Christian joy. We will see the underlying causes of joy, the outward effects of joy and many reasons to be joyful in the Lord. It will tell us the things we should take joy in and the things we should find glorious. It will realign our priorities to the things of most importance.

I began this book by describing how I preached on Philippians, only to find many people asking why it describes joy they do not have. One question I asked each person was, 'Would you say that you prioritize the kinds of things in your life that Paul and the Philippians take joy in?' Mostly the answer was 'No'. It is important for us to hear about these biblical priorities and decide to make them our own. We can only expect to know genuine Christian joy through radical Christian living. As we approach the sweeping panorama of joy in Philippians, we should hold two key ideas in mind:

- That we should glory in what the Bible glories in and find joy in the places it finds joy.
- That everything we discover must be worked out corporately in the body of Christ.

Joy-spotting in Philippians

A friend of mine recently went on holiday to the Scilly Isles. He told me that the number of birdwatchers on the islands was almost overpowering! These committed enthusiasts dashed this way and that across the islands to spot and document birds and sat for hours waiting for the briefest glimpse of something rare, often only to go home disappointed.

Thankfully, discovering joy in Philippians is nothing like the frustrating and laborious job of spotting rare birds. It's difficult *not* to spot instances of joy, the book is so full of it. For the remainder of this chapter I want to give a quick overview. Stop now and read through Philippians. It's only four chapters, so you can do it in half an hour.

The foundation for joy

Philippians 1:21 is the most important verse for understanding Philippians as a whole, and the best way to approach what it says about joy:

> For to me, to live is Christ and to die is gain.
> (Philippians 1:21)

Although the verse doesn't mention joy, it tells us Paul's overriding aim for the whole of his life and death. Everything he is and all that he does is for the sake of Jesus Christ. Paul wants his life to be passionate about Jesus in every possible way. Compared to Jesus, there is nothing of remotely similar value in life or in death – in this world or the next.

This is the force of his two statements. 'To live is Christ' tells us that Jesus is the whole of his life, the very measure by which all other things are valued. 'To die is gain' is, for me, one of the most challenging statements in the whole Bible. It says that when we lose absolutely everything else, if we have Christ, then we still gain. If we compare the value of everything else in life with having Jesus Christ and being with him in heaven, if we put all we have on one side of the scales and only Jesus on the other side we discover that he infinitely outweighs it all. Therefore he is of more worth than all the rest. Having him is better than having all the rest, and knowing him is infinitely more joyful than having all the rest.

This is why Philippians 1:21 is the foundation for joy in the Christian life. Joy is always related to Jesus. There is no Christian joy that doesn't come from knowing him, worshipping him and finding hope in him. There may be *happiness* in other things, but not lasting joy, because all other things are secondary, mediocre and short-term compared to him. If we substitute joy in Christ for happiness in other things, then we settle for second best.

Confidence in Jesus brings joy

Let's move on to some verses that actually do talk about joy and see how this confidence in Jesus works. The first reference to joy is:

> I thank my God every time I remember you. In all my prayers for all of
> you, I always pray with joy because of your partnership in the gospel

from the first day until now, being confident of this, that he who began
a good work in you will carry it on to completion until the day of
Christ Jesus.
(Philippians 1:3–6)

Paul is joyful that the Philippians are Christians. They share in the
good news of Jesus. He is thrilled when he thinks about them,
because God has done the same work in their lives that he has done in
Paul's. His joy is compounded by the assurance that his Philippian
friends will continue to know God working in them, all the way
through to completion at Jesus' second coming. This is much more
than mere good friendship. It is Jesus-centred, cross-saturated friendship that leads him to rejoice in God because of them.

Paul writes about two situations that may appear, on the surface,
to damage the good news. The first is that he is in prison; the second,
that a few people in Philippi have started preaching with a motive to
criticize and disparage him. They are saying things like 'Paul's a
hopeless witness for Jesus. He's locked up like a common criminal. It
would be much better for you Philippians to be under our teaching
than his, because he has made Jesus look disreputable by getting
arrested.'

Paul replies, 'It is just not like that. I am in chains for Christ'
(1:12–14). As a result of his chains the whole palace guard heard the
good news (about 12,000 men!) and lots of Christians had been
encouraged to be more gutsy in their witness for Jesus. Furthermore,
in response to his critics, Paul recognized that the message they
preached was the correct one, even if the motive was unwholesome.
So despite all the hardship, the good news was being preached. This
was by far the most important thing, and so Paul was joyful about it,
regardless of his circumstances:

But what does it matter? The important thing is that in every way,
whether from false motives or true, Christ is preached. And because of
this I rejoice.
(Philippians 1:18)

Even his prison situation paled into insignificance compared with
this wonderful reality. Whether he lived or died for Jesus, Paul was

completely confident that he would be delivered, that he wouldn't be ashamed of what he had believed and lived, and that he would be given courage to exalt Jesus. So he continued to rejoice:

> Yes, and I will continue to rejoice, for I know that through your prayers and the help given by the Spirit of Jesus Christ, what has happened to me will turn out for my deliverance. I eagerly expect and hope that I will in no way be ashamed, but will have sufficient courage so that now as always Christ will be exalted in my body, whether by life or by death.
> (Philippians 1:18–20)

He felt caught between two wonderful options. If he died in Christ's service, then he would go to be with Jesus, which would be amazing. But if he remained alive, he could do more fruitful labour and stay with the Philippians. The reason he wanted to stay was their joy and Christian growth. Notice how the two are linked:

> Convinced of this, I know that I will remain, and I will continue with all of you for your progress and joy in the faith, so that through my being with you again your joy in Christ Jesus will overflow on account of me.
> (Philippians 1:25–26)

In other words he wanted Christians to know growth and joy in Jesus, and would do whatever he could to ensure that it happened.

Finding joy in fellowship with other Christians

The church in Philippi was a good church. They witnessed clearly to Jesus, they were united with the apostles and they showed great generosity to missionaries. However, it wasn't without its problems. One problem was that people were falling out. One case was bad enough to warrant a specific mention in 4:2, where Paul pleaded with two women, Euodia and Syntyche, to put their differences aside and work together for the gospel as they had before. So bad was their quarrel that he asked a third party to step in and help the women sort it out. It all sounds sadly contemporary and realistic.

The problem of Christians falling out is a big theme in the letter. Paul counteracts it, not by demanding good behaviour (which would be an argument from law), but by appealing to them to have the same attitude Jesus has:

> Who, being in very nature God,
>   did not consider equality with God
>   something to be grasped,
> but made himself nothing,
>   taking the very nature of a servant . . .
> (Philippians 2:6–7)

He adds that because Jesus humbled himself to rescue us, God has given him the greatest honour of all. One day everyone will bow to him and admit he is Lord. Because of this Christians should tremble, realizing that we serve a Saviour who was once lowly but is now great. This attitude leads to the end of complaining and arguing among Christians. When this happens, Paul rejoices:

> But even if I am being poured out like a drink offering on the sacrifice and service coming from your faith, I am glad and rejoice with all of you. So you too should be glad and rejoice with me.
> (Philippians 2:17–18)

Faith in action leads Christians to hold out the gospel towards each other with good attitudes. Their attitudes show that the gospel is true and that their faith is real. Of course this brings joy – it shows that Jesus is Lord! In Philippians 1:3 Paul thanks God with joy because the Philippians are *his* partners in the gospel. Now he rejoices because they are partners with *each other*.

Finding joy in missions
When Christians work *together* in witnessing to Jesus with one heart, one mind and with godly attitudes to each other, the result is powerful mission. The Christians in Philippi were only a small group, but they took a disproportionately large interest in world mission. They were concerned for Paul's mission, they sent out missionaries of their own, and they wanted the message about Jesus to be heard all over the world. It's great to be part of a church like that. Mission should be a top priority for all churches. When it slips from being a

priority, a church is in decline. As Dr John Piper comments, missions exist to make worshippers:

> All of history is moving toward one great goal, the white-hot worship of God and his Son among all the peoples of the Earth. Missions is not that goal. It is the means. And for that reason it is the second greatest human activity in the world.[1]

The goal of missions is worship. Missions gather the people of God from every corner of the world, seeing them converted by the preaching of the good news, taken from darkness to light, from idolatry to godliness, from hell to heaven. No wonder the church in Philippi was keen on missions. And no wonder Paul says that missions bring great joy. It brings joy to the *missionaries* when churches are taken up with the great task:

> I rejoice greatly in the Lord that at last you have renewed your concern for me.
> (Philippians 4:10)

It brings joy to the *churches* when missionaries are faithful in their task:

> Welcome him [Epaphroditus] in the Lord with great joy, and honour men like him, because he almost died for the work of Christ . . .
> (Philippians 2:29–30)

And most of all it brings joy to the *Lord*. Paul says of the gifts the Philippians sent for mission:

> They are a fragrant offering, an acceptable sacrifice, pleasing to God.
> (Philippians 4:18)

God is pleased with sacrifice for the sake of missions. It brings him joy, because it shows concern for his glory above our material comfort. This is why the Bible says that we rejoice in suffering. It is not that suffering in itself is good, but that suffering for the sake of the Lord and for the good news produces Christian character, to God's great glory.

Joy in the Lord is a safeguard against false teaching

One further theme in Philippians is that enjoying God is a safeguard against false teaching that would fatally damage Christian joy:

> Finally, my brothers, rejoice in the Lord! It is no trouble for me to write the same things to you again, and it is a safeguard for you.
> (Philippians 3:1)

The exhortation to rejoice is a safeguard from the legalists who would like the Christians to be circumcised and to obey the law. Paul says, 'Watch out for them – they are joy-stealers. If getting circumcised isn't enough to steal your joy in itself, then bear in mind that joy is found only in the Lord, and they would subtly like to take you away from his gospel of grace.' Paul boldly proclaims that the legalists' message is futile rubbish and loss compared with knowing Christ, which is surpassing greatness (Philippians 3:7).

Children never give up goodies willingly. Try to take sweets from children and you have a fight on your hands. But offer them something better, and they have very short-term memories for what they previously considered so valuable. This is why rejoicing in the good news is a safeguard against legalism. When we taste and see that the Lord is good, when we stand under the overflowing fountain of his grace and find it irrepressible and irresistible, when we discover his joy welling up in our hearts by the Holy Spirit, then we will not want to return to legalistic religious duty.

We must regularly teach ourselves these things, read about them in the Bible, find good books about them and rejoice together in them. The Philippians knew about grace and joy, but still needed to be reminded as a safeguard. We are not yet at the end of our life's journey, and it is not impossible for us to be distracted, beguiled and lured away from grace by sweet-sounding religion. If we let that happen, we will fling away our joy in order to embrace rubbish. Paul wants to safeguard our hearts. He wants us to know Christ, to revel in him and trust him alone, to press after him and take hold of him, to forget what is behind and strain for the prize for which Christ has called us heavenwards.

Philippians is a letter about the joy of the *Lord*. We find joy in godly priorities because it is joy in the Lord. These are the things of

God and the activities that please him. They are the outflow of the grace of God and the expression through godly relationships of the character of God. When we look for joy in these things, we find it, because they are God-things – and he is overflowing with joy.

Philippians both starts and ends with grace from the Lord Jesus. Paul prayed for it and anticipated that God would pour it into the lives of the believers. They knew the same Lord and the same grace we can know. We have the same hope of heaven that they had. We live two millennia later, but God has not changed. He still overflows with extravagant grace to all who believe, and in provision of joy for all those who live, love and witness out of hearts brimful with that grace. Glory in the Lord Jesus, worship by the Spirit of God, put no confidence in the flesh – and rejoice!

Questions

1. Paul finds joy in the following godly things: confidence in Jesus, partnership in the gospel, the good news being preached, missions-focused churches, godly Christian relationships.

   Which of these do you most need to pursue? How might you start to do so this week?

2. Should Christians expect to know joy if they are not interested in these things? Why, or why not?

3. Try to correct these misquoted verses from Philippians *before* looking them up to see what they actually say:

   > The important thing is that in every way, whether from false motives or true, Christ is preached. But when people do it with false motives I am furious.
   > (Philippians 1:18)

   > But even if I am being poured out like a drink offering on the sacrifice and service coming from your faith, I am personally scared and fear for all of you.
   > (Philippians 2:17)

4. Memorize Philippians 3:7–10 this week.

Notes

1 J. Piper, *Let the Nations Be Glad* (IVP, 2003), p. 20.

6 Rejoice in God

Noel Edmunds, the well-known TV presenter, once said that the most boring thing Britain has to offer is church. I don't know what sorts of churches he had been in, but they obviously made a poor impression. The popular media stereotype of church is of a boring hour on a Sunday morning, where incomprehensible men in fancy dress offer irrelevant, inaccessible messages and meaningless rituals to uninterested people. Church-as-cough-medicine: you know it is good for you because it is unpleasant, but you can't wait for it to be over.

This caricature is as far away from real, joyful, grace-saturated Christianity as it is possible to get. Yet the world must have received the idea from somewhere. Is it possible that we Christians have sometimes been guilty of public joylessness, concerned to be faithful but not to be engaging, to proclaim truth but not to be visibly thrilled and gripped by it? The reality that Noel Edmunds and so many others are blind to is that the gospel of Jesus Christ is the source not of dullness but of joy. Inasmuch as churches and Christians have ever given the impression that things are otherwise, then we have not grasped hold of the wonderful promises of passages like Philippians 1 or Romans 5 or Galatians 3. We will delve quickly into Romans 5 before returning to Philippians.

In this chapter I want to encourage you to be elated at taking joy in God and to reckon on the truthfulness of his promises in your life. As I am writing I am praying that you will find him replacing any joyless frame of mind and heart with joy in his truth, as you treasure his promises.

A glorious answer to a terrible crisis

Helpful reading: Romans 5

Romans 5 begins with 'Therefore'. It's an old (but useful) cliché that whenever we see a 'therefore' in the Bible, we should stop to see what it is there for. Here is the story so far:

- In his introduction to the letter Paul summarizes the good news and his desire to visit the Christians in Rome. The introduction finishes in 1:16 with the claim that the gospel is the power of God to save everyone who believes in Jesus, and is not something to be ashamed of.
- Then comes a section setting out how the whole world is in rebellion against God. This section finishes in 3:9–20 with the assertion that there is nobody in the world good enough for God. Everybody is sinful, condemned. And this is a BIG problem.
- Next comes a glorious section with the BIG answer to the BIG problem. The answer is that although we are helpless, unable to rescue ourselves, make ourselves good, or come to God by our own power or strength, God himself has made it all possible. He has done it by sending Jesus to die as a substitute for us, becoming sin for us so that we can receive God's righteousness. What good news! And not only does the gospel provide forgiveness, it also provides many other benefits from God that accompany forgiveness.

This is where Romans 5 picks up the story. And what a story it is! It is bursting with all the benefits that come from God to people who believe in Jesus. The high point is the final verse:

just as sin reigned in death, so also grace might [will] reign through
righteousness to bring eternal life through Jesus Christ our Lord.
(Romans 5:21)

One astonishing benefit of the gospel is that sin and death no
longer reign over Christians. Instead it is *grace* that reigns *through*
righteousness. In other words, grace triumphs for Christians by God
declaring us righteous and acquitted because of Jesus. And it reigns
in order to bring eternal life through Jesus. Christians reign in life by
receiving grace.

No longer God's enemy

Romans 5 begins by revealing a great truth about the status and
identity of Christians. It says that, because we are justified by faith
(not by works, not through law), we have peace with God. Peace is
something the world craves and it is in short supply. But we have the
peace that matters most – we are no longer God's enemies.

A friend emailed me recently to say he thinks biblical teaching that
says non-Christians are God's enemies is disgusting and reprehensible.
He told me forthrightly that the idea of hell puts God on a level with
Saddam Hussein, producing obedience by fear. He said that my own
belief in hell lumped me in with Saddam too.

Lots of people think that way, but they are wrong. They
incorrectly assume that people are all fundamentally morally good,
even if they choose to ignore God. But they aren't. A schoolteacher
friend of mine explains it excellently when she says that the child in
her class who is seemingly inoffensive but who consciously ignores
the teacher is just as much a rebel as the deliberately offensive child.
The first child cannot claim she is neutral simply because she doesn't
break up the lesson or bully others. She is as disobedient as the
second. In the same way the Bible is clear that ignoring God while
claiming to be good is not OK. It is illegitimate to claim that we are
not against God if we ignore him. It is an affront to his authority and
his name. God loves his name above all things. He is jealous for his
name. His name is his renown in all the world, and he considers it to
be the most important thing. God will not be defamed!

Even in terms of flawed human justice we instinctively understand
that defaming someone, or taking away their rightful reputation, is

wrong. How much more wrong is it to defame the infinite reputation and worth of God? He is defamed by the deliberate act of rebellion and equally defamed by those who, like the schoolchild, simply ignore him. The defamation of God makes us his enemies and puts everybody on earth under his rightful punishment. But God's punishment is not reprehensible, as my friend claimed, because God has freely given his own Son to provide reconciliation and pardon to all who will accept it. But here is the rub for my friend: we *have* to come to God this way – there is no other way. We cannot come as we please and expect or demand acceptance. This is the opposite of the world's desire for self-empowerment. It is utterly dependent and completely humbling, but the result is worth it: we have peace with God through Jesus. Far from the relationship being one of terrified obedience through fear, on the level with obeying Saddam Hussein out of dread, it is one of peace, faith and grace. There *is* fear in the Christian life, but it is the fear of magnificent awe, not of dreadful punishment. Having peace with God, we are set free to enjoy God, which is part of what Romans 5 describes as 'reigning in life'.

Rejoicing in God
Romans 5 urges us to rejoice in three things:

- the hope of the glory of God (5:2)
- our sufferings (5:3)
- God (5:11)

We will look at this last one here and the other two in the next chapter.

For some Christians, even the vocabulary of rejoicing in God may come as a surprise. Fearing God, obeying God, understanding about God, these may be more familiar thoughts. But *rejoicing* in God? That implies not just acknowledging his being and his truth, not just understanding about him, but knowing him and subjectively engaging with him. However, rejoicing is the language the Bible uses. It is inadequate and unbiblical for us to acknowledge that the Bible speaks about joy but at the same time be satisfied without experiencing it.

We enjoy the things we treasure. If we do not rejoice in God when the Bible instructs us to, then we may be failing or refusing to treasure him. That is hardness of heart and stubborn sin to be repented of.

When we repent of hardness of heart and seek God, we begin to value the reality of his promises. It can be a little like waking up. We become conscious once again of receiving his grace and it turns into praise rising in our hearts. Look again at how Paul describes it:

> For if, by the trespass of the one man, death reigned through that one man, how much more will those who receive God's abundant provision of grace and of the gift of righteousness reign in life through the one man, Jesus Christ.
>
> (Romans 5:17)

Rejoicing through Jesus Christ

Romans 5:11 tells us that we rejoice in God *through* our Lord Jesus Christ, an act made possible because we have received reconciliation with God in him:

> Not only is this so, but we also rejoice in God through our Lord Jesus Christ, through whom we have now received reconciliation.
>
> (Romans 5:11)

'Do you want to know joy in God?' asks Paul. 'Then dwell on Jesus Christ. Fix your mind on him. Let the eyes of your heart be absorbed with him.' The thing that should most absorb us is what Jesus accomplished on the cross; that is, bring about our reconciliation with God. We will know joy and be released in our spirits to rejoice if we do.

The *Saturday Times* has a section called 'Body & Soul'. This week's edition contained articles on heart disease, fresh fruit, sex and why French women stay slim. Why the title mentions the soul, I do not know. We live in an age that values 'spirituality' as long as there is no clear definition of what that means. In the last few weeks I have seen and heard the word used to describe dieting, Eastern mysticism, visiting health spas and gardening! Anything, in fact, that you feel subjectively nurtures your inner contentment and happiness. Even Jesus can have a place in contemporary secular spirituality, as long as he is a Jesus who makes us feel good and doesn't make demands on us. A Jesus who is happy to take his place as one part of a 'Body & Soul' spiritual pick and mix, alongside aromatic candles, pleasant recreational activities and interesting cultural experiences.

That kind of Jesus is a useless and pathetic idol of our own creating, on a level with pagan idols of wood and stone. Pathetic because there is no connection between that Jesus and reality, and useless because we are the ones who can decide what we would like him to be for us. The one thing that the Jesus-idol of contemporary spirituality never does is challenge us to be reconciled to God. It merely affirms that we are OK as we are. There is no joy through reconciliation in that.

I am fascinated by the reactions of non-Christians to the good news about Jesus. Even in the 1980s most believed that science had buried God, that he doesn't exist. We hear that much less nowadays. Instead we hear that 'Jesus is true for you and that's great, but my options and choices are OK for me and that's great too' (subtext: 'Don't you try to make me listen to what you want to say about Jesus').

But the other options aren't OK. It is not all right for us to let people avoid hearing about Jesus, because only in the cross of Christ is there reconciliation with God. And, therefore, only there do we find lasting, eternal joy in God. The other options are not just second best, heading in a vaguely good direction, but not as good as what Christians have. They are heading in the *wrong* direction, because unless people are reconciled to God, everything they think is bringing them happiness will one day prove to be short-lived and inadequate. They will face judgment without the reconciliation that comes through Jesus.

Avoid the worship of earthly appetites
How should we live out this joy in reconciliation? Let's return to Philippians to put some flesh on the bones.

> Join with others in following my example, brothers, and take note of those who live according to the pattern we gave you. For, as I have often told you before and now say again even with tears, many live as enemies of the cross of Christ. Their destiny is destruction, their god is their stomach, and their glory is in their shame. Their mind is on earthly things. (Philippians 3:17–19)

These verses describe people who are living out the *opposite* of joy in God, the opposite of the way we are to live. They seek joy in their appetites. Stomach-worshipping of this kind is the obsession of much

REJOICE IN GOD | 93

of contemporary life. Body image is a worship-object in our culture. Adulation of drink, sex and TV practically defines what 'a good time' means for many. When a glossy magazine eulogizes about (slim, French) 'sex-gods and goddesses' it reduces worship to a matter of gut and groin.

The people Paul warns the Philippians about were taking pleasure in shameful things. The pleasure of this world is the rival in human hearts to knowing joy in God. The word 'glory' is significant. These people are not just innocently enjoying the good things of the world, of which there many. It is their attitudes that give them away. They place their trust and their whole understanding of pleasure in legalistic religion and their own self-righteousness. They are worshipping idols of religious duty, cultural purity and food laws.

Externally this might seem different from our contemporary world's objects of worship, but inside it is exactly the same. They have set their minds on earthly things. The things they value are mere earthly show. They expect that this will win them approval from God. People today may focus on different objects, but the temptation to equate earthly things with blessing is the same. It happens in the 'Body & Soul' section, but it can happen in churches too. This is especially true of churches that teach prosperity, but it is just as present in *anything* that displaces the grace of God and the crucified Christ in our affections.

Who can honestly claim that we never let a relationship, a new stereo system, a dieting plan, an exciting vacation or any of 101 other things displace God for a time? There are many things that are not wrong in themselves but that become wrong when we set our minds on them and desire them above God. He becomes nothing, belittled and defamed. The earthly things replace him.

Live according to Paul's pattern

Paul's answer to this is to live according to the pattern he gave (verse 17), and take note of others who model it. We must live as people who know the cross of Jesus, taking joy in reconciliation. The worst thing about the non-Christians here is that they are enemies of the cross. They were denying reconciliation. This denial can be subtle and religious, or bold and secular, but it is still denial. These people were not neutral towards God; they were enemies.

If we are not reconciled, we are enemies of the cross. The only way to escape being an enemy of the cross is to be reconciled to God *by* the cross. Paul continues by comparing enemies of the cross with real Christians:

> But our citizenship is in heaven. And we eagerly await a Saviour from there, the Lord Jesus Christ, who, by the power that enables him to bring everything under his control, will transform our lowly bodies so that they will be like his glorious body. Therefore, my brothers, you whom I love and long for, my joy and crown, that is how you should stand firm in the Lord, dear friends!
> (Philippians 3:20 – 4:1)

What a difference! We live differently because we

- are citizens of a different kingdom – heaven;
- have a different Lord – Jesus;
- have a different hope – resurrection and heavenly things.

All this is bought for us by the cross. There is no message of hope other than the cross. The true Christian never tires or gets bored of the cross or wants other things to displace it. It is the centre of our joy because there Jesus achieved our reconciliation.

Saved through the cross, living through the cross

Galatians says the same thing. We discover in Galatians 3 that the Christians were *converted by* believing what they heard, but also that they *go on* with the Holy Spirit by believing what they heard. The vital message they had heard and believed was this:

> Before your very eyes Jesus Christ was clearly portrayed as crucified.
> (Galatians 3:1)

> Christ redeemed us from the curse of the law by becoming a curse for us, for it is written: 'Cursed is everyone who is hung on a tree.' He redeemed us in order that the blessing given to Abraham might come to the Gentiles through Christ Jesus, so that by faith we might receive the promise of the Spirit.
> (Galatians 3:13–14)

May I never boast except in the cross of our Lord Jesus Christ,
through which the world has been crucified to me, and I to the
world.
(Galatians 6:14)

All the blessings come through the cross. There is nothing worth
boasting about except the cross. The message is utterly cross-centred
because reconciliation is utterly cross-centred.

Spot the difference

Perhaps the scariest thing about the non-Christians in Philippians 3,
is that they try to look like Christians. They are not obvious God-
haters but have a great show of religion. They want everyone to
perform religious duty like they do. But they put their confidence in
their duty and not in the cross, and that marks them out as enemies
of the cross. I recently heard a churchman speaking on the TV.
An interviewer asked him, 'What is the greatest strength of your
church?' He replied, 'The greatest strength and only hope for my
church in times of division is our ability to listen to all regardless of
their belief.'

I don't know the state of that man's heart before God, but I do
know the danger of that kind of answer. It places hope in diversity
and allowing an assortment of beliefs. It is likely to value that
diversity above the message of the cross when people disagree. It
is likely to glory in good relationships rather than reconciliation
with God. It sounds well meaning, even kind, but there is no real
relationship to be had in churches between the believer and the one
who denies the cross. One is reconciled to God; the other trusts
churchmanship, attendance at the prayer meeting, confession,
charity, denomination or any number of other things subtly sub-
stituted for grace. Trusting in these other things suffocates any hope
of joy in God.

Pressing on to heaven

Christians – take joy in God! Dwell on reconciliation. We are to live
only for the sake of Christ. We must put his interests first and
subordinate everything else to the gospel. Knowing Jesus is greater
than anything else. Everything else is literally rubbish when put

beside knowing Christ. We want to be found in him, not having a shabby righteousness of our own, but his perfect righteousness before God. Living under the shadow of the cross of Jesus Christ is the only place to find joy in God, for it is the only place where there is the hope of heaven. Listen to Paul's language about going forward in the Christian life:

> Not that I have already obtained all this, or have already been made
> perfect, but I press on to take hold of that for which Christ Jesus took
> hold of me. Brothers, I do not consider myself yet to have taken hold
> of it. But one thing I do: Forgetting what is behind and straining
> towards what is ahead, I press on towards the goal to win the prize
> for which God has called me heavenwards in Christ Jesus.
> (Philippians 3:12–14)

I haven't yet got it all – I press on, forget what is behind, strain towards what is ahead, push towards the goal. All of us who are mature should take hold of this. There is a prize waiting. Are you running the Christian race in such a way as to win the prize? That prize is Christ. He is the goal. He is the reason God has called you heavenwards. You can almost sense Paul standing on tiptoe, really wanting us to get hold of this.

Our home is in heaven and our joy is God himself. When we forget this and settle down as if this world is our home, we inevitably seek our joy in the wrong place. The values of this world conform us to its expectations and second-rate dreams. God's desire and design for Christians is that we should have our eyes on the prize, and that we should live as though we really want it. Let's live in this world for the sake of heaven, putting the gospel first, considering everything else to be rubbish in order to enjoy Christ's unending riches.

Questions

1. In what kinds of things do people around us seek joy? What sorts of joy do those things bring?
2. Imagine a non-Christian says to you, 'How can you possibly say that everything is rubbish compared to Jesus?' What would you say in reply?

3. Complete the blanks in the following verse:

> For if, when we were _____, we were _____
> _____ through _____, how much
> more, _____, shall we be _____
> _____! Not only is this so, but we also _____
> _____ through our Lord Jesus Christ, through whom we
> have now _____.
> (Romans 5:10–11)

4. Now list everything these verses tell you about the status of Christians. If you are a Christian, praise God for each one with joy! If you are not yet a Christian, isn't it time you took these things to heart and received God's gift of reconciliation through Jesus?

7 Rejoice in the benefits of Christ

The fundamental assumption of this book is that Jesus Christ is the centre of all things. The Bible says that God the Father has raised him from the dead, seated him in the place of power and authority over creation and declared that every knee will bow in homage and recognition before him. The Father rejoices and delights in the Son.

However, the Bible takes an utterly remarkable further step. We find it explained in Ephesians 1:22:

> And God placed all things under his [Jesus'] feet and appointed him to be head over everything *for the church*, which is his body, the fulness of him who fills everything in every way.
>
> (Ephesians 1:22, emphasis mine)

It is an astonishing verse. Follow the logic of it. God has made all things subject to Christ. Jesus is the conquering victor and ruler of everything. That is the strength of 'all things' being placed under his feet. The Father decreed, 'My Son is the head, the sovereign majesty, over all things.' But then he added, 'My Son will exercise that authority on behalf of the church, in order to bless it.'

To those who say church is boring, irrelevant or inconsequential in the Christian life we should reply, 'No! The church of Jesus Christ is glorious and holy. It is bought by his blood and engaged to the Lord. Despite all its faults, the church is the vessel into which God has poured his infinite kindness and the means by which he shows his grace to the world and the heavenly places (Ephesians 2:6). He is pouring out blessings of being united to Jesus, for the church to enjoy.'

The church is intimately united with Jesus. She is the body; he is the head. She is the bride; he is the bridegroom. He has died for us and we have died with him. He is our substitute, sacrifice, mediator, prophet, priest and king. So close is the relationship between Jesus and the church that the Bible says our life is now hidden with Christ in God. We are new creatures, with a new life, new fellowship, new motivation in the grace he has given us, and new priorities, of which the first is to glory in God.

God delights to bless

A group of young Christian leaders has met regularly for training in our house over several years. Recently one member was leaving the group. Before she left, she said to my wife, Ros, and me, 'I would like to come round for an afternoon and spend some time cleaning your house as a thank you for all I have received here (and for all the mess the team leave behind!).' We ran a whole gamut of emotions: She has spotted the house isn't clean! She probably thinks we are filthy! Oh no, we are going to have to say 'Yes' even though we are Brits who don't receive grace well! Then we asked why she wanted to do it. Her reply was wonderful: 'I know you aren't expecting anything, but I would like to do it just because I want to bless you. I've been thinking about how I can bless you and this seemed like a good, personal way.' She wanted to bless us just because she wanted to bless us. She was modelling grace to us. We were thrilled.

The Bible is full of lists of blessings God heaps on those who are united to Jesus Christ. Sometimes we can get a little suspicious of this because the world doesn't behave that way. In the world we get what we pay for and we work for less than we think we deserve. When offered something free and undeserved, we want to know if there is a hidden cost, or when the payback will be demanded. Sometimes we might have an inkling that God's blessings seem too good to be true.

Sometimes we can respond to grace out of a kind of inverted humility that says, 'I am not good enough to have you do that for me, so I couldn't receive your gift.'

But that is exactly what we mustn't do with God. The moment we say 'I'm not good enough, so I won't receive' or 'What is the cost of receiving this gift that I will pay back at a later time?' we fall straight into legalism. We don't receive the blessings as blessings, or the grace as grace, because deep down we think, 'God can't possibly act that way towards me.' If you think like that (and all of us do from time to time), here is a vital thing for you to remember and treasure: He does! He does it because you are in Christ. He delights in Christ and therefore he delights in you. He is pleased to do you good and to bless you, and it all rebounds to his glory as he is seen to be kind to sinners out of pure, free grace.

Five snapshots of blessing

We could look at *lots* of Bible passages that spell out the wonderful benefits of being in Christ that we should cherish and enjoy. I have decided to keep to Philippians because of its great emphasis on rejoicing in the blessing and glorying in God. In the rest of this chapter I want to look at five brief snapshots of blessing, following Paul's sequence in his letter.

Blessing snapshot 1: Take joy in confident belief
I hated being lined up to be selected for football teams at school. Team captains would pick in turn from the most to the least able footballers. Being terrible at football, I was always last and even then was usually chosen reluctantly. Most team captains would rather have left me to cheer on the touchline. I usually agreed with them, but on the odd occasion I recall desperately wishing I was just good at football. I wished I commended myself to the captains. Better still would have been to be so good I could practically choose which team I would like to be in and in which position on the field.

Philippians 1:29 tells us that Christian belief is not a human decision.

> For it has been granted to you on behalf of Christ not only to believe on him . . .
> (Philippians 1:29)

However much we would like to commend ourselves to God, or however good we try to be, there is no option to choose yourself to be a Christian. We are completely dependent on God choosing us. However, God is not like the team captain who chooses the good, the charismatic, the fast and the strong. He does not have a list in his mind that he works through systematically from the most acceptable to those who are barely across the line. Indeed God always goes the opposite way, as Paul says in 1 Corinthians:

> But God chose the foolish things of the world to shame the wise;
> God chose the weak things of the world to shame the strong. He
> chose the lowly things of this world and the despised things –
> and the things that are not – to nullify the things that are, so that
> no-one may boast before him. It is because of him that you are in
> Christ Jesus . . .
> (1 Corinthians 1:27–30)

Becoming a believer is not dependent on human wisdom or strength. It does not rely on your background or your family connections or where in the world you are born. It is not dependent on a feeling you had at an evangelistic meeting, or your good deeds, or your current experience of living a successful Christian life (however you try to measure success). No, God chose! As Paul put it in Philippians 1, it has been *granted* to you to believe on him. It has been given to you. The team captain has chosen the unlikely to be believers. All the initiative in your becoming a believer was down to God. God decreed, 'That person will become a believer,' and, by whatever mechanism he chose for us to hear and respond to the good news, we did. He set his grace upon us when we were his enemies, and that grace invincibly came through for us.

Therefore we should be joyful in believing, because belief doesn't originate with us – it is a gracious free gift of God, to us, in Christ. Because belief doesn't come from us, we are secure. If you have a Bible open, you might be thinking that Philippians 1:27–29 doesn't speak about joy, but rather about fearlessness, fellowship and faith. That is right. However, Philippians 1:3–6 does expand on the joy that accompanies this security that Christians have in Jesus:

I thank my God every time I remember you. In all my prayers for all of you, I always pray with joy because of your partnership in the gospel from the first day until now, being confident of this, that he who began a good work in you will carry it on to completion until the day of Christ Jesus.
(Philippians 1:3–6)

We can be confident that God will keep us going as Christians to the end, because faith comes from God and not from us. He *has* started a good work by saving us and will *continue and complete* that work through gospel transformation in our lives right up until the day Jesus returns. Indeed Philippians says that it is granted *on behalf of Christ*, which means faith is given for Jesus' sake. When the world and the heavenly powers see God-given Christian faith, then Christ receives glory because God's gospel so obviously works. And when Paul thinks of his gospel partners, people transformed by this free grace of God, he prays with joy:

It is right for me to feel this way about all of you . . . [for] all of you share in God's grace with me.
(Philippians 1:7)

If you are a believer, put your confidence in God today – and rejoice!

Blessing snapshot 2: Take joy in righteousness and the fruit of righteousness
Society is increasingly target-driven. Profit is the bottom line in almost every workplace. A number of years ago I was a clerk in a high-street bank. Over a three-year period I watched as the ethos in the banking world changed from a customer-driven approach that emphasized personal service, customer care and a friendly environment to a ruthless product- and target-driven approach. Products were specified for sales targets in any one month. A list of sales for each staff member went up on a notice board. High performers were publicly congratulated, but woe betide anyone who came bottom of the sales list. Effectively driven to compete against each other for their jobs, employees went from being highly motivated to insecure and

depressed, from feeling loyal to their employer to seeking any opportunity to leave.

The underlying message in many areas of contemporary life is that our value is determined by our achievement. We can be proud of high-volume sales or sporting success or the attainments of our children. We should be humiliated and dismayed by less than high-quality performance in any area of life. In a world that believes we are what we do and we are what we own, our very identity is threatened by the fear of underperformance.

When we translate this mentality into the Christian life, the result is legalism. It is all too easy to trust our performance because we believe it is measurable, maybe not in absolute terms but at least against how everyone else is doing. 'I might not be perfect, but I don't gossip like her'; 'I've led more Bible studies than him and I serve regularly behind the coffee counter after church, so that the congregation think I am an appropriately humble-minded servant.' This is an attempt to gain a sense of value and worth by what we do. An attempt to make ourselves good. The Bible calls it shabby righteousness, on a level with dressing ourselves in filthy rags.

Paul's journey from legalism to freedom. Before he became a Christian, Paul was a performance-driven legalist, or, as he put it, someone who put confidence in the flesh:

> If anyone else thinks he has reasons to put confidence in the flesh,
> I have more: circumcised on the eighth day, of the people of Israel,
> of the tribe of Benjamin, a Hebrew of Hebrews; in regard to the law,
> a Pharisee; as for zeal, persecuting the church; as for legalistic
> righteousness, faultless.
> (Philippians 3:4–6)

That is quite a catalogue of things for which he used to congratulate himself. By any standards of the day he was the bees knees, the ultimate high flyer. He did *everything* right. He was faultless and was heading for the top.

So what was the problem? When Jesus met him, as he travelled to Damascus to persecute the Christians, he discovered that *legalistic* righteousness isn't, in fact, righteousness at all. It's no good. All his previous attempts to establish that he was right with God, whether through his perfect heritage or his perfect performance of religion, were worth precisely nothing. In fact they were worth less than nothing because they fooled him into thinking he was doing OK when he wasn't.

However, to Paul's delight, he discovered that everything he had striven so hard to achieve and that couldn't be achieved through human effort – namely, being right before God – was given to him as a free gift by Jesus. This earth-shattering revelation instantly threw everything else in life into a perspective that showed it up as useless compared to the righteousness Jesus gives:

> But whatever was to my profit I now consider loss for the sake of Christ. What is more, I consider everything a loss compared to the surpassing greatness of knowing Christ Jesus my Lord, for whose sake I have lost all things. I consider them rubbish, that I may gain Christ and be found in him, not having a righteousness of my own that comes from the law, but that which is through faith in Christ – the righteousness that comes from God and is by faith.
> (Philippians 3:7–9)

There are three big contrasts here:

- *The things Paul previously counted to his profit* versus *Christ.*
- *Everything in the whole world* versus *the surpassing greatness of knowing Christ.*
- *A righteousness from ourselves (in Paul's case by law), which is no righteousness at all* versus *righteousness that comes from God and is by faith.*

They add up to a very strong exhortation to us: Christ is better than the world, so seek your righteousness in him and from him. Ask him for it and receive it from him. Consider everything else less than useless compared to him.

Paul previously had confidence in his heritage and his religious duty. They were his daily delight. After meeting Jesus, he had no confidence in them at all. Indeed to boast in them after becoming a Christian would take glory away from Jesus. It would make it look as if Paul could add something to all Jesus had done for him. We too find it easy to trust other things and try to measure our Christian progress by them. Don't do it! They are less than worthless. They distract us from Christ. They need to be repented of. We can enjoy righteousness by faith or we can trust other things that destroy our righteousness and kill joy. We cannot do both.

Paul's antidote is clear and simple: when we are faced with temptation to find our righteousness in other things, we should *rejoice* and *beware*:

> Finally, my brothers, rejoice in the Lord! It is no trouble for me to write the same things to you again, and it is a safeguard for you. Watch out for those dogs [who put confidence in the flesh] . . .
> (Philippians 3:1–2)

In other words, be careful not to be led away from your righteousness because you will also be led away from your joy. Rejoice in having Christ's righteousness given to you. Do so actively and out loud! Rejoicing in the truth will guard your heart from the joylessness that comes when we turn from the truth.

Making progress in the faith. If having righteousness from Christ is meant to bring us joy, so is our progress in the faith. Paul says that his aim, if he is spared death, is to remain with the Philippians for their 'progress and joy in the faith' (1:25). He is right to expect progress, because faith grows. God will complete the good work he has started in us.

In my garden there are a dozen raspberry canes. We planted them two years ago and now they are bearing a lot of fruit. In the summer we pick raspberries almost every day and, from just a dozen plants, have far more than we can eat. They are good canes. This week my father took a chainsaw to a pear tree in his garden. 'It isn't a good tree,' he explained. 'It calls itself a pear tree but it just doesn't produce pears.' You can tell a good tree from a bad one by what it produces.

People who try to gain their own merit or righteousness are like that pear tree in my parents' garden. There is no fruit from their righteousness. Those who live out the righteousness of Christ, on the other hand, are like the raspberry canes – pleasing, fruitful and delightful!

Paul says:

> And this is my prayer: that your love may abound more and more in
> knowledge and depth of insight, so that you may be able to discern
> what is best and may be pure and blameless until the day of Christ,
> filled with the fruit of righteousness that comes through Jesus Christ –
> to the glory and praise of God.
> (Philippians 1:9–11)

His expectation is that Christians are filled with the fruit of
righteousness and that God is glorified because of that fruit. Philippians explains what the fruit of righteousness looks like in our
lives, in our faith, in our witness and in our relationship with other
Christians. In the two verses above, the fruit of righteousness is
connected to the love that flows from us to other Christians because
we have first experienced God's love. Paul wants Christians who
grow in love. Not a wishy-washy love, but love that abounds in
knowledge of God and insight into his ways. It leads to purity and
discernment and victory in the battle against sin. Christians who love
like this live lives that glorify and praise God. Paul prays for them
with joy:

> I thank my God every time I remember you. In all my prayers for all of
> you, I always pray with joy . . .
> (Philippians 1:3–4)

We should pray for the fruit of righteousness and desire it in
our lives with joy. God is being glorified. We are being sanctified as our
love leads us in the ways of God. Exhibiting the fruit of righteousness
means we make progress in the faith and God is adored.

Blessing snapshot 3: Take joy in the prize ahead
The English have a huge victim complex when it comes to sport. As I
write this, the England football team have just been knocked out of a
major tournament because of a dubious decision by a referee. At least,
England fans think it was a dubious decision. Only in this way can
we protest our sporting prowess and moan about other countries. We
didn't lose: we were unfairly treated. At the same moment the great

hope of English tennis has failed to win Wimbledon. Again. And the rugby squad, though wonderful in the 2004 World Cup, have been lamentable ever since.

The problem with the way the English follow sport is that we set unrealistic expectations. The newspapers decide before the competition that our team or player is the greatest and that nothing less than total victory will ever satisfy us. In this way we can make even great performances seem like national disasters just because our players didn't go all the way to lifting the trophy.

The English are particularly ungracious when it comes to sporting defeat, but it is not wrong in itself to be motivated by prizes. Prizes provide focused goals and govern our behaviour. The athlete who wants to win the Olympics tomorrow will train as much as possible today to maximize his physical ability. Paul says that there is a prize ahead for Christians:

> [I have not already been made perfect] but I press on to take hold of that for which Christ Jesus took hold of me. Brothers, I do not consider myself yet to have taken hold of it. But one thing I do: Forgetting what is behind and straining towards what is ahead, I press on towards the goal to win the prize for which God has called me heavenwards in Christ Jesus.
>
> (Philippians 3:12–14)

Paul lists three wonderful things that make up this prize: resurrection from the dead (3:11), citizenship in heaven (3:20) and the gift of a resurrection body from Christ. The prize sounds almost too good to be true. But it is true and it is worth working towards. Listen to the verbs Paul uses to express how worthwhile it is to obtain this prize: 'I *press on*'; '*forgetting* what is behind'; '*straining* towards what is ahead'; 'to *win*'. Why is he so urgent? Why so unremitting? Because these are the very things Jesus has died to win for us, the very purpose of God for Christians, the reason he has elected us and called us towards heaven (3:14).

When the world thinks about Christianity the last things to spring to most people's mind are glory, escape from death and citizenship in heaven – the home to beat all homes. On the whole, Christians are not very good at being enthusiastic about these great things we are certain are coming. No wonder people don't always find Christianity attractive. If they haven't heard about this hope, then they haven't heard about the real thing. If they haven't seen Christians who glory and take joy in the prize, then they haven't seen the reality in action.

Philippians 3:12–14 does not explicitly state that we are to take joy in the prize, but it is there. Philippians 3:18 states the opposite case:

> For, as I have often told you before and now say again even with tears, many live as enemies of the cross of Christ. Their destiny is destruction, their god is their stomach, and their glory is their shame. Their mind is on earthly things.
> (Philippians 3:18–19)

This tells us that we glory in what we set our minds on. If our mind is set on earthly things, then we glory in them. By contrast, if our mind is set on the prize, then we glory in the prize. Paul has said this very thing earlier in the chapter:

> For it is we who are the circumcision, we who worship by the Spirit of God, who glory in Christ Jesus, and who put no confidence in the flesh . . .
> (Philippians 3:3)

We *glory* in Christ Jesus. We *glory* in the prize. What does it mean for us to glory in something? My dictionary says, *to exult with triumph, rejoice proudly; to render glorious, to invest with glory or radiance; to extol, honour, magnify with praise.*

Those are three good categories of definitions:

- *To exult.* To take joy in God. To boast in him. To glory in a person or prize is to adore. To let our heart well up in admiration because we find the person so admirable.
- *To adorn the things we glory in.* When we glory in God and take joy in the benefits of Christ, we reflect his beauty and magnificence back to him. All praise and worship is therefore adornment of what God has already done. When we say we glorify him, what we are actually doing is reflecting his own glory back to him through our delight in him.

- *To amplify and increase the honour God has from others.* If we glory in someone, we rightly want them to be famous, so they receive the honour due them, not just from us but from all people. Therefore evangelism and missions are the outflow of our glorying in God. We enjoy him, glory in the prize and rightly want others to do so. We take the gospel to all nations in order that God may be known and glorified.

Take joy in the prize. Glory in it. Worship God for it. Set your heart on it. Ponder it, describe it to yourself and revel in it. And describe it to others all over the world so that God becomes famous for what he will do for Christians.

Blessing snapshot 4: Take joy in a changed heart and attitude
Everyone who has been a Christian for a little while knows that churches are not always places of contented fellowship. There are often issues that bubble away, barely concealed beneath a veneer of pleasantness. There are doctrinal issues such as a church's position on speaking in tongues or modes of baptism. There are practical issues about church activities, the youth, worship styles or leadership decisions. Sometimes there are plain personality clashes.

Just in case you thought that any of these are new things, one of the main reasons Paul wrote to the church in Philippi was to sort out similar issues. Good Christians were bickering. Two women, Euodia and Syntyche, who had previously worked in evangelism with Paul were now scratching each other's eyes out. Paul was grieved by this and was determined neither to let the issues continue nor to sweep them under the carpet.

Instead he appealed to them to resolve their differences on the basis of joy in God.

I plead with Euodia and I plead with Syntyche to agree with each other in the Lord ... Rejoice in the Lord always. I will say it again: Rejoice! Let your gentleness be evident to all. The Lord is near.
(Philippians 4:2–5)

There is a connection between dealing gently with others and joy. When we rejoice in God and our sights are set on him, then our hearts are changed. We appreciate that he is close and we know he is transforming us. How then can we continue to fight fights and hold grudges when we know how gracious and kind he has been to us and how he continues to renew us every day? We learn this clearly from Philippians 2:

> If you have any encouragement from being united with Christ, if any comfort from his love, if any fellowship with the Spirit, if any tenderness and compassion, then make my joy complete by being like-minded, having the same love, being one in spirit and purpose. (Philippians 2:1–2)

The power of such rhetorical questions is the little words 'if' and 'then'. Computer programmers have a basic tool called an 'if–then' statement. When the program runs, it checks to see *if* a certain condition is fulfilled. If it is, *then* it subsequently runs a further set of instructions. That is exactly what is going on in these verses. *If* these things are true of the Philippians and us, *then* we *must* do the things that follow on from them. Being like-minded with each other, having love for one another, being one in Spirit and purpose are not optional for people who are united with Christ, comforted in his love and who desire to be tender and compassionate as he is. They are obligatory as the perfectly natural consequence of being like Jesus. We love because he first loved us. This was his attitude and it will be ours if we wish to be like him:

> Your attitude should be the same as that of Christ Jesus. (Philippians 2:5)

Sometimes we refer to sharp-edged people as 'having an attitude'. It is rarely complimentary. It usually means they have an abrasive character, that they are blunt with others and keep a nasty temper on a hair trigger. How is your attitude? Are you like that or are you like Christ? You cannot be both. Your attitude displays the inclinations and motivations of your heart. If you are a person 'who has an attitude', then your heart is not renewed as it should be, and it will affect your relationships with other Christians. Bad attitude is often applauded by society. It is the very lifeblood of TV interviews. But it must be repented of by Christians. The attitude of Christ is not bombastic, proud, short-tempered or rude. It is the attitude that caused him to make himself a servant and to die on a cross for the salvation of others.

Paul appeals to us to make sure our love is growing and our attitudes towards other Christians are being transformed by that love. This, he says, brings joy to him (2:2, 17) and glorifies God (2:11). Indeed it makes his joy complete, because he can see the likeness of Jesus being formed in his friends before his eyes. He can watch them glorifying Jesus in their hearts and behaviour. He can witness relationships moving from ungodly conflict to Christ-adoring unity and love.

Blessing snapshot 5: Take joy in suffering for Christ
We see from Philippians 1:29 that God has granted us belief in Jesus and that this is a cause for joy. The other clause in the verse is much more shocking to today's comfort-driven Western world:

> For it has been granted to you on behalf of Christ not only to believe on him, but also to suffer for him, since you are going through the same struggle you saw I had, and now hear that I still have.
> (Philippians 1:29–30)

That is an outrageous, an almost impossible, statement. It is a verse over which I hesitate to write, aware of just how deep and traumatic suffering has been in the lives of some of my friends. We all recognize that there is suffering in life, but this verse is much more than just a recognition of the reality of universal suffering. It says it has been *granted* us to suffer for Christ, and that grant is for Christ's sake or on Christ's behalf. Which means that the suffering is a grace. It is intended by God, it is deliberate and it is good news to us.

How on earth can this be true? How can suffering be a grace? How can God want us to suffer – and for that suffering to be glory to him? How is suffering a benefit of being in Christ?

Before answering these questions, one point of clarification is necessary. Today's world is overshadowed by the ghastly threat of global terrorism. We are beginning to see a clash of values at the level of whole civilizations. To simplify greatly, on the one hand the material-driven West does not understand value or religion-driven cultures; on the other hand religious cultures often make a direct connection between Western wealth and spiritual bankruptcy and moral degradation. One tragic phenomenon that reflects the inability of these mutually exclusive world-views to speak to each other is the growing use of suicide (or homicide) bombers as terrorist weapons. Our society in Britain is utterly uncomprehending of why someone would become a suicide bomber unless they are noticeably evil, brainwashed or insane. We have spent so much time and effort adding to our material wealth and comfort that the idea of suffering for something, let alone dying for it, is totally outside our mindset. Our automatic assumption is that there is nothing worth jeopardizing our individual comfort for to that degree. The upshot is that when the world hears about people who think that a cause is worth dying for, it reaches for words like 'fundamentalist', 'fanatic' or even 'terrorist' to describe the threat it believes such an attitude represents.

Let's be clear. The good news of Jesus is worth suffering and dying for. He is of more value than life itself. And that puts all real Christians into a category Western societies do not understand, and therefore feel threatened by. However, the suffering to which we are called as Christians, for the sake of Christ, is *utterly* different from the suffering and death of the suicide bomber. We follow the man who died for his enemies. Our suffering is not that we are prepared to kill for our beliefs – nothing could be more contrary to the good news. No, our suffering is that we are prepared to *be killed* for the sake of Christ and for the sake of taking the good news of Christ to the world.

How then can suffering be a grace? How can it be joy to us, as Romans 5:3 says it is. Let me give three short answers.

1. *Suffering for the gospel.* Suffering is a grace to us because we are suffering for the gospel. Our joy is not in any and all suffering: it is in suffering for the sake of Christ. When the Christians in Philippi suffered for living and telling the good news, Paul told them, 'That's exactly the same thing that is happening to me.' It is also exactly the same thing that happened to Jesus. The world hates Jesus and the good news and loves to persecute Christians. Gordon Fee puts it like this:

A crucified Lord produces disciples who themselves take up the cross as they follow him. We are thus to live *on behalf of Christ* in the same way Christ himself lived – and died – on behalf of this fallen, broken world. That is why salvation includes suffering *on behalf of Christ*, since those who oppose the Philippian believers as they proclaim the gospel of Christ are of a kind with those who crucified their Lord in the first place.[1]

This year I have watched as a university students' union in London turned on the community of Christians in the college with more vitriol than I have ever seen. 'Christians are cross-wearing mentalists,' proclaimed the union newspaper. 'I wish they would all go and crucify themselves. I would happily provide the nails.' The Christians had done nothing to deserve this, nor the subsequent threats of legal action against them or the freezing of bank accounts held with the students' union. For a brief while I feared for the Christian Union. It is a hard thing to face this kind of persecution for the first time, when life has previously been more comfortable. However, they reacted with exemplary faith, grace and quiet godliness. More than that, their persecution encouraged Christian students all around London to take a much firmer stand for the good news. Their response of faith was genuinely joyous to see.

When we suffer for Christ, it is a grace *because it is for the gospel.* It furthers the gospel, it confirms the truth of the gospel in us and is, in itself, a witness to the gospel as seekers watch how Christians endure the hatred of the world because the love of God is in us.

2. Suffering is a sign. Suffering for Christ is a sign for those who oppose Jesus that they will be destroyed and that we will be vindicated and saved (Philippians 1:28). By being prepared to suffer for Christ before the world, Christians make a powerful point that we believe in the God who rescues, even from death; we believe in heaven, hell and final judgment and we believe that the Lord will vindicate his people and judge all those who oppress them.

Not being intimidated in the face of suffering speaks about future certainties and unshakeable hope. It is a challenge to people who think that the future lies only in the grave and whose only hope is comfort now. It is also a challenge to those who believe that religious coercion or violence leads to future hope of salvation. We are not violent in pursuit of the gospel, but neither are we weak pushovers. No, Christians endure because of the reality of Christ in us by the Holy Spirit, and that enduring is a potent sign to the world.

3. *God uses suffering to produce Christian character.* Suffering for Christ is the tool of God for producing Christian character and hope in us:

> Therefore, since we have been justified through faith, we have peace with God through our Lord Jesus Christ, through whom we have gained access by faith into this grace in which we now stand. And we rejoice in the hope of the glory of God. Not only so, but we also rejoice in our sufferings, because we know that suffering produces perseverance; perseverance, character; and character, hope. And hope does not disappoint us, because God has poured out his love into our hearts by the Holy Spirit, whom he has given us.
> (Romans 5:1–5)

When we suffer for Christ, God produces in us the Christian virtue of perseverance. Steadfast pressing through. People who persevere under trial find that their characters turn to gold. All of us know of people who have an added dimension of depth, maturity and excellence because they have endured suffering in a godly way. They are becoming like Jesus in their character and are exemplary models for us to follow. That depth of character in turn produces hope. As we feast on Christ with our hungry hearts, our suffering makes us look to him and put our faith in him. When that happens we are changed by the Holy Spirit. So our hope doesn't disappoint us because we know God's love in our hearts, even at the darkest moments, by the Holy Spirit.

For non-Christians the opposite is true. Suffering doesn't produce character, because such people have no hope for the future. Life is bleak and ends in the grave. Suffering produces despondency; despondency, apathy; and apathy, despair. And despair disappoints utterly.

But not so for us! Our hope doesn't disappoint because God has poured his love into our hearts. We know his love and rejoice in it. It carries us through. While suffering for Christ is certainly not trivial or carefree, we nevertheless rejoice in it because it is a demonstration that God is preparing us for heaven.

Stand firm in joy

These five Bible snapshots show us that joyful living produced by faith, rejoicing in all the blessings of being in Christ and delighting in grace has real practical benefit. Our lives are transformed inside and out. Our hearts are renewed and so are our relationships. Our security and assurance of heaven are made more concrete as we are given strength to endure suffering for Christ. Lives like this are perfumed with the fragrance of heaven. They are attractive and beautiful.

Paul finishes the main part of his argument in Philippians with these words:

> Therefore, my brothers, you whom I love and long for, my joy and crown, that is how you should stand firm in the Lord, dear friends!
> (Philippians 4:1)

How do we stand firm? By rejoicing in the Lord! And then living out all the consequences of that joy. Paul tells us what to take joy in – all the benefits of being in Christ. If you know nothing of this joy, is it possible that you have never stopped to ask yourself whether Paul's joyous priorities are yours?

Questions

1. Which of the five snapshots of joy do you find you most easily recognize in your life? Which do you find hardest to recognize?
2. What would it mean this week for you to forget what is behind, strain towards what is ahead and press on to win the prize for which God has called you heavenwards in Christ Jesus?
3. Fill in the following blanks:

> I consider _____ compared to the surpassing greatness of _____, for whose sake I _____. I consider them _____, that I may _____, not having _____ that comes from the law, but that which is _____.

Now look up Philippians 3:8–9. If you made any mistakes, ask yourself the reason you made them. Are you believing false assumptions about the good news, which you need to unlearn?

Notes

1 Gordon D. Fee, *Philippians* (IVP, 1999), p. 81.

8 Rejoice in living and proclaiming the gospel

Like many churches, our church sends out and supports missionaries. Global mission is our heartbeat. Sending people to take the good news is part of the way we want to see God glorified all over the world. Back at home the church's mission strategy group does the unglamorous work of directing support, thinking strategically about world mission and helping the church to feel involved with everything that happens on the mission field. I suppose many churches have a similar group.

World mission should be at the heart of all churches because God is concerned to be glorified all over the world. However, the perpetual struggle is to make a concrete connection between what happens in the local congregation and what is happening in another country. One reason this sense of connection can be difficult to maintain is if we make an illegitimate distinction between church life on the one hand and mission and evangelism on the other. Church is what happens in the congregation on Sunday or in midweek groups. Evangelism is a separate category of special event or an activity reserved for specially gifted Christians or the vicar. World mission is even worse. To be a missionary requires the utmost dedication and sacrifice. We admire these people but secretly don't want to emulate them in case we end up somewhere uncomfortable.

This distinction between church and mission is neither helpful nor biblical. All it does is set up a divide between so-called 'normal' Christians and 'professional' Christians. Normal Christians live out their Christian lives in the workplace but would never see themselves as missionaries. Professional Christians get all the praise but need to be unusually gifted and dedicated to give up everything to serve God overseas. In setting up a distinction between the normal and the professional we also distinguish between Christian ministers (people with a particular anointing or ordination) and the laity (everyone else). Such divides reinforce false ideas about who does Christian ministry. The answer is obvious – the professional minister. They have the gifts and are paid to use them. All the rest of us receive ministry and get on quietly with our lives.

However, the Bible says that *all* Christians have gifts for some kind of service and promises that *all* Christians find joy in ministry. It is great to find some churches discovering afresh that the biblical pattern of church is that the work of the kingdom is done by all the people of God, not just the paid professional. If we make a distinction between normal and professional Christians, and conclude that normal Christians are not involved in ministry and mission, then we will neither look for opportunities to exercise our gifts nor experience the joy that comes from living the gospel. We might not have opportunities because our church deprives us of them, reserving service for the professional, or we might not have them because we turn down opportunities offered to us. Either way, living out gospel ministry brings joy for all Christians through their being directly involved in the work of God. Failing to do so is a joy-killer.

In Philippians Paul homes in on three aspects of living and proclaiming the good news of Jesus that bring joy:

- Living out the gospel with other local Christians.
- Living out wider gospel partnerships.
- Preaching the gospel.

1. Living out the gospel with other local Christians

We saw in chapter 7 that Paul claims that there is an inescapable link between knowing God and loving other Christians. The substance of that link is that born-again people have their hearts transformed by the Holy Spirit so that we become like Jesus in our attitudes. Here is how Paul describes those transformed attitudes:

Your attitude should be the same as that of Christ Jesus:

Who, being in very nature God,
  did not consider equality with God
    something to be grasped,
but made himself nothing,
  taking the very nature of a servant,
  being made in human likeness.
And being found in appearance as a man,
  he humbled himself
  and became obedient to death – even death on a cross!
Therefore God exalted him to the highest place
  and gave him the name that is above every name,
that at the name of Jesus every knee should bow,
  in heaven and on earth and under the earth,
and every tongue confess that Jesus Christ is Lord,
  to the glory of God the Father.
(Philippians 2:5–11)

We can instantly see that having a Christlike attitude makes it impossible for Christians to fight each other. If we do, then, by definition, we don't have the character of Christ. These verses pose the intimate questions 'What is my heart like? Is it Christlike today? Or are there evil things lurking there? Do I look inside and see Jesus-like humility? Do I want to sacrifice myself for Jesus and the gospel and the work of God in the lives of others? Or am I secretly proud? Or preoccupied with shameful things? Is my heart full of lies and gossip?'

Servanthood

We are to be like Jesus on the inside, with his values, thoughts, desires and motives. And we are to be Jesus-centred in everything we do. Paul would not have written these verses for the Philippians and for us unless there are dangers that churches and Christians might *not* conduct themselves in a manner worthy of the gospel. Being Christlike with other Christians means being a servant. Christian discipleship is servant discipleship, and Christian leadership is servant leadership.

The word 'servant' describes our *attitudes*. We can *pretend* to be servants because we know what is expected of us in church. We might know that if we want to be commended by others for being good Christians, there are certain things we can do to appear servant-hearted. But pretending to be a servant doesn't make us one, no matter what external acts we perform. Christ served others because he didn't grasp at status. His attitude determined his actions. He gave up everything and became obedient to death, and *therefore* was exalted to the highest place and given the ultimate name in order to bring glory to the Father.

This turns the world upside down. The world thinks that servant-heartedness is weakness. It despises the person who would rather be a servant than a master. Jesus said that lording it over other people is not a Christian pattern but a pagan one. He told his disciples:

> Not so with you. Instead, whoever wants to become great among you must be your servant, and whoever wants to be first must be slave of all. For even the Son of Man did not come to be served, but to serve, and to give his life as a ransom for many.
> (Mark 10:43–45)

Just in case we think servanthood sounds like setting ourselves up for misery in this life, let's remind ourselves that Paul says twice that it brings rejoicing in God (Philippians 2:2, 17). He rejoices to see practical Christlikeness in the Philippians, because through it God's character is seen in their lives.

Day-to-day Christlikeness
Paul goes a long way in Philippians to spell out what a Christlike attitude actually looks like in day-to-day life. Here is a summary list:

- Be like-minded (2:2).
- Have the same love (2:2).
- Be one in spirit and purpose (2:2).
- Do nothing out of selfish ambition or vain conceit (2:3).
- In humility consider others better than yourself (2:3).

- Don't just look to your own interests but also the interests of others (2:4).
- Do everything without complaining (2:14).
- Don't be argumentative (2:14).
- Be gentle (4:5).
- Think nobly (4:8).
- Follow Paul's example of godliness (4:9).

This is utterly countercultural. The world is selfish and cruel. You get on in the world by being the biggest, strongest rat in the race. Have it all, have it all now and have it at the expense of others. But not in the church of Jesus Christ. Paul won't have it. Jesus could have done that, but he didn't, and we are not to either. Instead we are to

> continue to work out our salvation with fear and trembling, for it is God who works in you to will and to act according to his good purpose.
> (Philippians 2:12–13)

We are living out what it means to be saved, depending on the purpose and power of God. We are a new community, an outpost of heaven. Bought by the blood of Jesus, we are to work together with other Christians with a single purpose – the gospel. We are to do everything we can to agree wholeheartedly with each other in the task of spreading the good news, for the glory of Jesus and the salvation of the lost. When we model our attitudes on those of Jesus, our behaviour becomes like his, and that is homage to him. He loves it when his people are like him.

Real fellowship and joy

Take a few minutes to cast your eye down the summary list above. There are several different kinds of exhortation:

- To work hard at being united in purpose with other Christians: be like-minded, have the same love, be one in spirit and purpose. How are you doing in these matters? Are you the one who loves to bring Christians together, or are you someone whose attitude is more likely to provoke others?

- To think correctly about yourself and other Christians: don't be selfish and conceited, think better of others than yourself, think nobly. How are you doing with these? Are they matters to rejoice about as you can see that God has been changing you? Or are they matters for repentance and reconciliation with others?
- To act correctly towards other Christians: look to other people's interests as well as your own, don't argue or complain, be gentle. If other people in your church were to tell you kindly and honestly how you are doing in these areas, what would they say? Do you want to be known for your kindness and peacefulness? Or are you notorious for your spikiness and short temper? Do people gravitate towards you for your loving thoughtfulness, or move away because of your quarrelsome nature?

Remember that these things are closely connected to Christian joy. Ask yourself whether you are conducting yourself Christianly at the moment? Are you standing alongside other members of your church, loving each other and working for the faith? Do you go home rejoicing in the truth after church on Sunday, determined to live it out at home, school or work, or do you go home to moan about the minister over Sunday lunch? Are you determined to live as a member of your church like a citizen of heaven should live, or is that not on your list of priorities?

Imagine two people sitting side by side in church. They are both engaged in the same Christian activities; they both attend services with equal frequency. Outwardly they look quite similar, but inside they are completely different. One is putting on a show. He knows what apparently Christian behaviour looks like. He is good at putting on a sham and gets a reward from the praise of people. But his heart is empty of joy because there is no real presence of God in outward acts of religion. The person sitting beside him might *do* exactly the same things, but be completely different inside. Her actions are motivated not by the praise of people but by submitting her attitudes to Christ and wanting him to be seen in them.

The irony of this illustration is that each person can think he or she is the other one! The godly person is likely to know her own flaws and internal sins only too well, and to feel keenly that she is often a sham. The ungodly is likely to identify his performance of religious acts (ceremony in some traditions, visible acts of service in others) as commendable godliness, thereby paying no attention to his heart. Good fellowship in a loving church should let us help each other over our natural self-deception, to pursue God together with genuineness, loving one another with truly open hearts. Changed attitudes lead to a deep desire for God and real Christian joy worked out in the daily surroundings of church life.

2. Living out wider gospel partnerships

What would you like your church to be well known for? Do you praise the quality of its teaching? Do you like to boast that its musical resources are top class or its history significant and important? The church in Philippi was well known for its exemplary partnership with people spreading the gospel around the world. The single thing that brings Paul the most joy in the life of the church at Philippi is partnership:

> I thank my God every time I remember you. In all my prayers for all of you, I always pray with joy because of your partnership in the gospel from the first day until now . . .
> (Philippians 1:3–4)

What is this joyful partnership in the gospel? What does it mean to be a gospel partner?

False unity

It is very common at the moment in the UK to hear Christians, churches and denominations talking about unity. 'Unity' is a big buzz-word, but it seems to me that the desire for it sometimes overrides the desire for accuracy, doctrine or truth.

To take one example, there are many initiatives in the UK at the moment to bring Catholics and some Anglicans into dialogue with each other, with a view to achieving common goals. Such dialogue takes place in other denominations too, but the move is especially noticeable in some parts of the Anglican communion.

Any initiative that aims at getting Christians talking to one other is commendable; but often such dialogue is maintained by downplaying doctrinal differences – sometimes even differences over vital things. In the Catholic–Anglican dialogue, for example, there are major issues of belief and faith at stake. Are we justified by faith alone or by a combination of faith and works? Is Scripture alone authoritative for Christians or is our authority a combination of Scripture and tradition interpreted by the Pope? Do we have unrestricted access to God in Christ or do we need a mediator in a priest? Do we pray only to God or also to saints and to Mary? The list could go on and all the differences are crucial.

One Christian leader recently said to me, 'If you think that those minor points of disagreement between Protestants and Catholics from hundreds of years ago are at all relevant to twenty-first-century Christianity, then you are dreadfully out of touch with reality.' He could not be more wrong. Those issues are so fundamental to how we are redeemed, how we live our Christian lives and how we understand the mission of the church that making sure our answers are biblical is the way we arrive at reality. Any attempt to enjoy an organizational appearance of unity without addressing such core matters is not unity at all. Lowest-common-denominator unity is not partnership in the gospel.

Real unity
Real unity never avoids the uncomfortable issues. A little while ago I spent a morning with the godly leader of a mission agency. I knew this leader spends a lot of time trying to bring others together in genuine, deep gospel partnerships, and that in doing so always asks the question 'Is it possible to work with this or that group and maintain my orthodox witness?'

That is the right question. I was simultaneously shocked and delighted, therefore, when he asked it of me and the ministry of which I am a part. With disarming and godly frankness he said, 'I have an issue with you that, currently, is preventing me from pursuing gospel relationship with you. Can we talk about it?' What an invitation! Intimidating? Yes! Uncomfortable? Definitely! But an open door to step beyond the superficial, to let my defences down and get real about the gospel. We talked through the morning and he put his finger on a negative aspect of my ministry that had significant consequences for his own. Had he not taken the risk, I would have had no opportunity for repentance and no opportunity for further fellowship. But, praise God, he did, because he wanted to go forward together in the gospel.

Where there is no agreement about the gospel between partners, there is no gospel partnership. Wherever we find people putting aside the gospel to promote unity, there is no gospel partnership. On the other hand when we find brothers and sisters who will confront us, like I was confronted that day, there is an excellent opportunity for developing gospel partnership.

Partnership in the gospel

The partnership Paul has in mind is exactly partnership *in the gospel*. He continues his letter:

> It is right for me to feel this way about all of you, since I have you in my heart; for whether I am in chains or defending and confirming the gospel, all of you share in God's grace with me.
> (Philippians 1:7)

Gospel partnership is sharing in gospel work with gospel people everywhere, so that the gospel goes to the world. It is sharing the work of God with all others who know the grace of God. This, says Paul, creates joy in his heart and affection between the partners. They enjoy the same aims; their unity is not in superficial matters but in central ones.

How actively do you share in the work of the gospel with others around the world? How is your church doing in this area? It is a common misconception that world mission is an advanced sphere for Christians to get into after they have everything else sorted out. The opposite is often the case. When we look away from ourselves in mission to the world, we tend to flourish in other areas of our Christian life. This should come as no surprise, because the good news going to the world is God's priority. It brings *him* joy, and therefore worldwide gospel partnerships bring *us* joy.

Timothy, Epaphroditus and Paul

Philippians gives three glimpses of the worldwide gospel partnerships the church enjoyed: partnership with Timothy (2:19–24), with Epaphroditus (2:25–30) and with Paul (especially 4:10–19).

Timothy and Epaphroditus were both well known to the church. They had sent Epaphroditus to find Paul in prison and give him a gift. Paul in return hoped to send Timothy as a messenger to the church and receive news back from them through him. Both men are examples of normal, faithful Christians. They demonstrate vibrant Christian living, but there is nothing unattainable about their work. Paul uses them as illustrations of the kind of Christian life he expects everyone in the church in Philippi to live.

We learn that Timothy was concerned for the interests of Jesus Christ above his own interests (2:21). This flowed out in his taking an interest in the welfare of the Philippian church (2:20) and his working in the gospel alongside Paul (2:22). This is the normal expectation for those who put the interests of Jesus first, that we take an interest in the witness of others and that we do the work of the gospel ourselves.

Epaphroditus was sent to take care of Paul's needs. He is described as 'my brother, fellow-worker and fellow-soldier, who is also your messenger' (2:25). What a lovely description! We have an insight into his character, vision and hard work for Jesus. There was also a tenderness to Epaphroditus. He became ill in the service of Christ, but wasn't distressed for himself but for the Philippians in case they became too worried on his behalf (2:26). He longed for them and cared for them. His attitude was the same as Paul's, in fact, who longed for them with the affection of Christ (1:8).

Because of his illness, Paul sent Epaphroditus back to Philippi. He instructed the church:

> Welcome him in the Lord with great joy, and honour men like him, because he almost died for the work of Christ, risking his life to make up for the help you could not give me.
> (Philippians 2:29–30)

Epaphroditus deserved an honourable, joyful welcome. The kind of partnership he demonstrated is at the heart of Christian living and should be at the heart of every church. Being involved in what God is doing globally through gospel partnerships brings joy in the work of God, and joy in the workers too. When we hear reports and stories of what God is doing all over the world to bring himself glory by rescuing sinners, that should be a great delight and cause a buzz in our churches.

The Philippians also had a partnership with Paul. Their personal concern for him brought him joy: 'I rejoice greatly in the Lord that at last you have renewed your concern for me' (4:10). It also brought joy to God: 'I am amply supplied, now that I have received from Epaphroditus the gifts you sent. They are a fragrant offering, an acceptable sacrifice, pleasing to God' (4:18–19). And it also brought supernatural abundance to the Philippians themselves: 'And my God will meet all your needs according to his glorious riches in Christ Jesus' (4:19).

This was an excellent partnership. There was nothing superficial about it. It was so much deeper than churches merely agreeing to have joint meetings and claiming that they therefore have partnership. Paul and the Philippians had joy together in God. They shared the same concern for the good news to go to the world. They met each other's spiritual and practical needs and rejoiced in each other's work for the Lord. It is a great example of what a church should look like when it is functioning properly in gospel partnerships.

Gospel partnerships and you
Let's ask some practical questions about this. Do you resonate with this theme of worldwide gospel partnerships? Who do you have this kind of partnership with? Can you list several people? Who does your church enjoy this kind of mutual support with in the work of the gospel? How can your partnerships be developed, improved and made more active and effective? How much air time do such partnerships have in your meetings? How much public exposure is given to world mission? I sometimes visit a church that has recently decided to dedicate some time in services to describe the life and witness of faithful missionaries. Two weeks ago they considered Jim and Elisabeth Eliot. What a great idea! What percentage of your giving or your church's budget goes towards wider gospel partnerships? The thing that first attracted my wife and me to our current church was the clear desire to dedicate as large a percentage of income as possible to world mission. We believe this often indicates that a church has right priorities, a focused gospel vision and joy in God.

Gospel partnerships are an area of Christian life in which we can let our imaginations run riot as we try to think up the most creative, most extravagant, most thoughtful and helpful ways to honour the work of the gospel and workers for the gospel. In the mission I work for a frequent question is 'How can we honour the staff? How can we bless them and love them and appreciate them?' These are the right questions. In the answers there is abundant gospel joy for the giver and the receiver.

3. Preaching the gospel
The one single activity that drove Paul's entire life was proclaiming the gospel. It should drive all our Christian lives. Proclamation, as we shall see in a minute, is not reserved for the professional in the pulpit. It is for all Christians. Let's look at some verses at the start of Philippians:

> Now I want you to know, brothers, that what has happened to me has really served to advance the gospel. As a result, it has become clear throughout the whole palace guard and to everyone else that I am in chains for Christ. Because of my chains, most of the brothers in the Lord have been encouraged to speak the word of God more courageously and fearlessly.
>
> It is true that some preach Christ out of envy and rivalry, but others out of goodwill. The latter do so in love, knowing that I am put here for the defence of the gospel. The former preach Christ out of selfish ambition, not sincerely, supposing that they can stir up trouble for me while I am in chains. But what does it matter? The important thing is that in every way, whether from false motives or true, Christ is preached. And because of this I rejoice.
> (Philippians 1:12–18)

People were stirring up trouble for Paul in Philippi. They were raising their own profile by rubbishing him. But Paul wasn't very concerned by this, hurtful though it may have been. He knew God could easily use his imprisonment to ensure wider witness to Jesus. He can use ungodly authorities to make sure the word goes wherever he wants!

The part I find most astonishing is not the gentleness with which Paul corrects the gossip; it is the fact that he just didn't care about it.

Some of those with false motives were nevertheless preaching a correct gospel and Paul was so much more concerned about that than his own reputation that he was full of joy regardless of the personal smears. He didn't say, 'Well those people are proclaiming the gospel, so I will just have to put up with the situation.' Instead he said, 'People are proclaiming the gospel, and that makes me rejoice. Even if the motives are false, I still rejoice because the name of Jesus is being told around the world.'

The gospel is more important
This shows us how much more important the gospel is than anything else and that there is more joy from the gospel being preached than from anything else. How is this true? What makes the gospel more important and more joyful than anything else, even than personal reputation? We have seen the answer already. First, proclaiming Christ leads rebels to come to glory in Christ and to become true worshippers (3:2). Secondly, proclaiming Christ leads to progress and joy in the faith for believers (1:25).

God uses proclamation to lavish grace on us for conversion and subsequent growth. Do you want to see conversions? Speak the word of God fearlessly and courageously. Some people will hate you for it, but others will be gloriously rescued. The Bible says that angels rejoice in heaven when people repent and turn to God. No wonder we find it such a joy on earth. Do you want to see yourself and other Christians grow in grace and joy? Speak the word of God to each other. He uses it to shape his people. Some will call you 'super-spiritual' and 'too heavenly minded', but others will be refreshed and challenged and inspired to follow Jesus more whole-heartedly. They will stand firm when difficulties come, and their lives will be worship to God.

I said that proclamation is not just for the professional. We discover this in Philippians 3:

> Join with others in following my example, brothers, and take note of those who live according to the pattern we gave you. For, as I have often told you before and now say again even with tears, many live as enemies of the cross of Christ.
>
> (Philippians 3:17–18)

Paul has established a pattern for all Christians. The pattern is that we should do what Paul did. The opposite of the pattern is living as 'enemies of the cross of Christ'. We are not to live as enemies of the cross but are to proclaim the message. Observing his imprisonment, Paul says that

> most of the brothers in the Lord have been encouraged to speak the word of God more courageously and fearlessly.
> (Philippians 1:14)

The implication is that *all* of the Christians should be speaking the word of God, the message of the cross, courageously and fearlessly. Timothy did it, Epaphroditus did it and Paul did it. And Paul told all the Christians that they should be

> children of God without fault in a crooked and depraved generation, in which you shine like stars in the universe as you hold out the word of life ...
> (Philippians 2:15–16)

And of course we should all do it because Christ does it. He is holding out the word of life to this world. Are we going to do anything less? Paul proclaims this message over our plans and ambitions, our lives, families and churches: *Hold out the word of life!* Wherever you go and whatever you do, proclaim Jesus. There are many worthwhile things to do in life, but knowing God *is* life, both now and eternally when we die. That is how Paul can maintain that proclamation or preaching is more important and more joyful than anything else in life – because it is what brings abundant life through knowing God.

Does your church regularly teach you how to spread the gospel? If not, maybe it is time to ask your church leaders for some training on how to tell others the good news. It is time to pray that God will lead you into conversations at work or in your care home, or school, or on the golf course, that will bring life to people for God's everlasting glory and their everlasting salvation and joy.

Godly priorities
This chapter and the two preceding ones have all been about finding

joy through godly priorities for life. It is unrealistic to expect the joy the Bible speaks of if we don't prioritize the things it takes joy in. It is all wrapped up in Philippians 1:21, 'For to me, to live is Christ and to die is gain.' It is *all* Christ. He is the one in whom joy is found, now and when we die. You can try to emulate these things if you are not a Christian, but you won't find joy in them. You can try to use an illusion of these things to persuade people at church that you are living a full Christian life, but it will be a stifling burden rather than a joy if you are not pursuing Christ. You can think you are glorifying God by doing all the right things, but if you are doing them for their own sake to try to earn some merit, they are destructive of your joy.

Pursue godly priorities. Pursue the riches of Christ and don't be satisfied with less than he has for you. But first pursue him for himself. When we do we find there is godliness with contentment which is great gain (1 Timothy 6:6).

Questions

1. What does it mean to live according to the pattern Paul gave (Philippians 3:17)?
2. What changes do you need to make in your life in order to follow this teaching?
3. What changes might your church need to make to pursue the same godly priorities as Paul and the Philippians?
4. How personally involved are you in worldwide gospel partnerships? How involved is your church?
5. Does the thought of 'speaking the word of God courageously and fearlessly' fill you with excitement or dread? What sort of training would you like to receive from your church in order to help you proclaim Jesus?

9 Live by the Holy Spirit

I began this book with the story of some Christians who assumed that their Christian life is all a matter of duty. Some believed that their hard work or their knowledge was the measure of their Christian life. They rarely thought about joy, and when they did, they tended to think it is something to be experienced in heaven rather than on earth. What they learned from Philippians was shocking and challenging to them. It brought an aroma of an unfamiliar but wonderful reality.

Two questions have been the focus of this book: (1) If we lack joy in the Christian life, are we believing the gospel of unmerited grace? (2) And if we do believe the gospel of grace but still know little joy, is this because we fail to prioritize in our lives the biblical concerns that bring joy?

You may wonder if there is a contradiction between experiencing joy through unmerited grace and experiencing it through living in obedience to biblical principles. If we are meant to *do* certain things in order to experience the joy the Bible says there is in them, does this not contradict the enjoyment of God's unmerited favour? Is it not just re-establishing rules for joy, even though many texts teach we have died to the law with its lists?

It's a good question. Knowing joy is not a mechanical process in which we play no personal part. When we make sausages we put the meat in one end of the machine, crank a handle and sausages come out of the other end. In many conversations people have asked me if there is a mechanism for discovering joy. Is there a joy process, with guaranteed results, that works like the sausage machine? Can we submit ourselves to some kind of joy-making process, turn the handle of Christian-rules-for-joy, and become at the other end automatically, mechanically joyful? The very questions show how readily we desire sets of external rules.

A relationship with God

The answer to these questions is glorious and personal, and not at all mechanical. It isn't found in a list of things that earn God's favour, but through the new relationship Christians have with God. Jesus Christ is now the governing force in our lives. The Bible says he is our new husband with whom we are falling deeper and deeper in love.

When I was a student, I lived in a mixed-sex house with several others. One day the other male student and I noticed that a list of 'The Rules' had been posted on the kitchen door. They ran as follows:

1. The women make the rules.
2. The women don't tell the men the rules.
3. The men are meant to know the rules.
4. If the men don't act according to the rules they had better watch out.
5. The women may change the rules whenever they like.
6. The women may not tell the men when the rules are changed.

It was a good bit of fun. My male housemate and I never took it too seriously (and we hope the women didn't!). The Rules were a joke for a student house. Imagine, however, how I would feel now if my wife put up the list in our kitchen. Marriage doesn't work by rules but by love. It is rather more complex and relational than rules, but immeasurably better. I have a friend who explains that a relationship with God based on love rather than rules is a better relationship because love always does more than law.

So the question we must answer is a practical one: How do we live out this vital relationship in everyday life without turning it back into mere rules for obedience? We are very familiar with the terminology of 'having a relationship with God', but what do we mean by it?

The phrase the Bible uses to describe this reality is not 'having a relationship with God' (though this is a wonderful and important truth); it is to 'live by the Spirit' (Galatians 5:16). Sometimes related phrases are used: 'being led by the Spirit', 'serving in the way of the Spirit' and 'walking by the Spirit' or 'keeping in step with the Spirit'. Living by the Spirit is the means by which we enjoy obeying Christ in our betrothal relationship to him, and the way we make joy-filled Bible priorities our own without just making a new list of rules. We can try to do all the right things and experience no joy, if we are not doing them by the Spirit.

In this last chapter I will try to explain what it means to live by the Spirit and be led by the Spirit. Then we will look at how this works out practically in serving one another in love, growing in holiness and counting ourselves dead to sin.

What does it mean to live by the Spirit?

> But by faith we eagerly await through the Spirit the righteousness for which we hope. For in Christ Jesus neither circumcision nor uncircumcision has any value. The only thing that counts is faith expressing itself through love.
> (Galatians 5:5–6)

These verses teach that we don't yet have all the fullness of being made right with God. There is still a lot more to come when we get to heaven. In the meantime we have to wait. This wait is not frustrating, however, but full of excited anticipation because God's Holy Spirit is producing faith in us, making us certain of what we hope for and eager to receive it. The Spirit characterizes the wait, not with law (circumcision or uncircumcision), but with faith expressing itself through love. This is the heart of what it means to live by the Spirit: *that we live by faith, trusting the Lord for things we haven't yet received, and that our faith is worked out in love to others.* This is all the work of the Holy Spirit in us. Before the Spirit came into our lives we could not exhibit faith. He produced it in us. God sends the Spirit of his Son into our hearts, the Spirit who calls out, 'Abba, Father,' so that we are no longer slaves but sons and heirs (Galatians 4:6–7).

Normal Christian living

So, the Holy Spirit makes our relationship with our heavenly Father real. He calls out 'Abba, Father' in our hearts and makes us wait eagerly for the fullness of righteousness, all the time loving God and others out of faith. A Christian reading this should instantly think, 'But that is just perfectly normal, ordinary Christian living.' And that is exactly what it is! Living by the Spirit is not abnormal; it is normal. It is not mystical or magical, or vaguely defined and on a super-spiritual plain above other Christians. It is clear and basic.

A teacher of the law once asked Jesus which was the greatest commandment. He replied:

> 'Love the Lord your God with all your heart and with all your soul
> and with all your mind.' This is the first and greatest commandment.
> And the second is like it: 'Love your neighbour as yourself.' All the
> Law and the Prophets hang on these two commandments.
> (Matthew 22:37–39)

The emphasis in these verses is on the *all* and the *yourself*. If you wish to fulfil the law, you've got to love God with *all* your heart and *all* your soul and *all* your mind. It's not good enough to love God with 99.9% or be less than perfect to your neighbour, because sin still remains. If we wish to fulfil the law, we must obey it faultlessly in every part, all the time (Galatians 3:10; 5:3): an impossible task. But to break the law at any point means we are declared guilty.

However, Jesus has done what the law could not do. He has met its righteous requirements himself so that we can come to God and receive the Holy Spirit:

> Christ redeemed us from the curse of the law by becoming a curse for
> us, for it is written: 'Cursed is everyone who is hung on a tree.' He
> redeemed us in order that the blessing given to Abraham might come
> to the Gentiles through Christ Jesus, so that by faith we might receive
> the promise of the Spirit.
> (Galatians 3:13–14)

Hebrews says it even more clearly:

> For this reason Christ is the mediator of a new covenant, that those who are called may receive the promised eternal inheritance – now that he has died as a ransom to set them free from the sins committed under the first covenant.
> (Hebrews 9:15)

Following Jesus' perfect sacrifice to free us from slavery to the law, the Holy Spirit now produces righteous fruit in us. This fruit is seen in godliness of character and desire:

> But the fruit of the Spirit is love, joy, peace, patience, kindness, goodness, faithfulness, gentleness and self-control. Against such things there is no law.
> (Galatians 5:22–23)

The fruit of the Spirit does *not* come through obedience to the law. However, the external effects of the internal work of the Spirit may look curiously *similar* to law-keeping. He produces love for God and others. He is making our characters like Jesus'. In fact what the law anticipated in shadow form is the transformation brought by the Holy Spirit. The law was not sufficient to make us love God or others, but the Holy Spirit is:

> You, my brothers, were called to be free [from the law]. But do not use your freedom to indulge the sinful nature; rather, serve one another in love. The entire law is summed up in a single command: 'Love your neighbour as yourself.'
> (Galatians 5:13–14)

How can I live more experientially by the Holy Spirit?

Let's get really practical. We all have up and down days in our Christian lives. We all know the joy of special moments with God and the despair of slipping back into sin. We read about *living* by the Spirit, and it sounds like there is an active component to going on in the life of the Spirit. Is there something we can do that will help us to live by the Spirit?

The answer is 'Yes'. Paul says:

> Since we live by the Spirit, let us keep in step with the Spirit.
> (Galatians 5:25)

Here are two aspects to the Christian life:

- Live by the Spirit; prayerfully enjoy the Spirit producing faith worked out in love.
- Keep in step with the Spirit or be led by the Spirit.

How are we led by the Spirit? Paul says that it has to do with our desires:

> So I say, live by the Spirit, and you will not gratify the desires of the sinful nature. For the sinful nature desires what is contrary to the Spirit, and the Spirit what is contrary to the sinful nature. They are in conflict with each other, so that you do not do what you want. But if you are led by the Spirit, you are not under law.
> (Galatians 5:16–18)

And in Romans:

> Those who live according to the sinful nature have their minds set on what that nature desires; but those who live in accordance with the Spirit have their minds set on what the Spirit desires. The mind of sinful man is death, but the mind controlled by the Spirit is life and peace.
> (Romans 8:5)

The Holy Spirit creates desires in us and sin creates desires in us. We can choose to focus our minds on one or the other. We can see that being led by the Spirit has to do with our desires when we compare Romans 8:5 and Galatians 5:25 (see Table 1 opposite).

We are changed from the inside out. God has transformed, and is transforming, our desires. If we want to walk more closely with the Holy Spirit, then we will set about desiring what the Spirit desires and denying what our sinful nature desires in all the decisions of the day. The Spirit is within us and desires to obey God. We could not

Galatians 5:25		Romans 8:5
Since we live by the Spirit	equals	Those who live in accordance with the Spirit
let us keep in step with the Spirit	equals	have their minds set on what the Spirit desires

Table 1

experience this new desire before we became Christians. All we knew was a strong desire to disobey, even if we dressed it up in an outward show of morality. Now we have a strong desire to obey. The Spirit achieves the goal of the law in us (something the law itself could never do) by changing us, not with an external list, but by transforming our hearts and attitudes.

The Spirit gives power over sin in the Christian life. As Paul puts it:

So I say, live by the Spirit, and you will not gratify the desires of the sinful nature.
(Galatians 5:16)

For many years I read this important verse the wrong way round. I *thought* it said, 'Make sure you do your best not to gratify the desires of the sinful nature. Make every effort not to do certain things, go certain places or think certain thoughts, and the exercise of that effort is walking by the Spirit.' My wrong understanding led me to believe that I could deny sinfulness by my own human effort. But that is just self-reliance. If we read the verse that way it leads us to attempting to gain our own righteousness and victory over sin by sheer effort.

Fortunately this verse doesn't say that – it says the exact opposite! When we live by the Spirit, he replaces our desires for sin with desire for God. He might do it slowly and not all at once, but he is doing it. The result is that the desires of the sinful nature are displaced and recede progressively into the distance. That is not to say that they don't sometimes re-emerge to try to trip, accuse and condemn us, but the Spirit is progressively sanctifying us by making us desire God. He *has* made us perfect for ever and *is* making us holy:

by one sacrifice he [Jesus] has made perfect for ever those who are
being made holy.
(Hebrews 10:14)

Can we take the credit?

If we set our minds on what the Spirit desires, is this not a human
work for which we can take credit? Instead of measuring our success
by our obedience to the law, can we now measure it by how much
faith we exercise, or how good we are at setting our minds on what
the Spirit desires?

We so easily slip into wanting to do things to validate ourselves
rather than receiving God's forgiveness and acceptance as a gift. We
can even try to turn faith into a work. Paul won't let us get away with
it. When we look closely at our new-found godly desires, we discover
that underlying them all, like a foundation underlies a building, is the
work of the Holy Spirit in our character. However much we dig
away, trying to find some deep godly desire that comes from us rather
than from God, we always discover that his foundation is deeper.
There is nothing good in us that he hasn't already put there, no act of
faith that he hasn't prompted and empowered. As Peter says:

His divine power has given us everything we need for life and godliness
through our knowledge of him who called us by his own glory and
goodness.
(2 Peter 1:3)

Our desires to be led by the Spirit are therefore grounded not on
our ability but on God's transforming work in our hearts. The lovely
fruit of the Spirit is the basis of our new behaviour, and is all produced
by God. My friend Derek Cross explains that we don't bring fruit to a
fruit tree. It is an insult to an apple tree to believe that you have to
put apples on it for it to be fruitful. In the same way we don't bring
the fruit to our Christian life; it is grown by the Holy Spirit. *Acting
in faith is therefore not a work of ours but a joyful recognition of a work of
God*. It drives us not to take the credit but to give thankful praise for
grace.

Let me summarize it like this: The Holy Spirit came to live inside us
when we became Christians. He is transforming us from the inside

to become like Jesus Christ. He does this by producing his fruit of godliness in our characters. This fruit in turn causes us to desire godliness that we could not desire and did not want before. Recognizing and receiving this grace and following these strong new desires for God is what the Bible means by 'keeping in step with the Spirit' or 'being led by the Spirit'. Being led by the Spirit is the way that the power of sin in our lives is broken, to be replaced with a whole new orientation to God. The result in our lives is wonderful:

> May the God of hope fill you with all joy and peace as you trust in him, so that you may overflow with hope by the power of the Holy Spirit.
> (Romans 15:13)

So trust him. Put your faith in him. Pray for him to produce more and more godly fruit in your character and to strengthen your new, godly desires even further. It is the way to overflowing hope, peace and all joy.

How do we serve one another in love?

Being led by the Spirit means that Christians serve each other in love. We see this connection in Galatians:

> You, my brothers, were called to be free. But do not use your freedom to indulge the sinful nature; rather, serve one another in love. The entire law is summed up in a single command: 'Love your neighbour as yourself.' If you keep on biting and devouring each other, watch out or you will be destroyed by each other.
> So I say, live by the Spirit and you will not gratify the desires of the sinful nature.
> (Galatians 5:13–16)

Living by the Spirit has this corporate dimension. It leads to the opposite of 'biting', 'devouring' and 'destroying' each other: serving each other in love.

Pause for a moment to ask yourself if you find any of your own behaviour challenged by these verses. You cannot be led by the Spirit and refuse to love your brother or sister in Christ. It is impossible to live by the Spirit and bite and devour other Christians. They are mutually exclusive. Do these verses tell you anything that you need to repent of? If you do so, *that* is being led by the Spirit. If you decline, then you are denying the power and authority of the Spirit in your life.

How do we serve each other in love in the power of the Holy Spirit? The key word is 'love', the fruit that the Spirit produces in transformed character. See just how close the connection is in Paul's mind between this fruit of God in our lives, and our behaviour, positively and negatively, towards other people:

> But the fruit of the Spirit is love, joy, peace, patience, kindness,
> goodness, faithfulness, gentleness and self-control. Against such things
> there is no law. Those who belong to Christ Jesus have crucified the
> sinful nature with its passions and desires. Since we live by the Spirit,
> let us keep in step with the Spirit. Let us not become conceited,
> provoking and envying each other.
>
> (Galatians 5:22–26)

The Holy Spirit is producing fruit in the lives of Christians. If we cannot identify anything in this list of fruit in our own lives, then we need to pray to God for it. He is also getting rid of desires that belong to the old nature that produce evil fruit in our characters. We have crucified the sinful nature so we don't follow its passions and desires anymore. We are keeping in step with the Spirit. The consequence is that we must not be conceited, must not be people who provoke and we must get rid of envy in our lives and our churches.

'Negatively' the Spirit throws a spotlight on to attitudes and actions that are in contradiction to us serving each other in love. He convicts and empowers us to repent of them and get rid of them. We are to throw off things that stop us loving other Christians. It might be a hard and lengthy process, but it starts with putting ourselves under God's authority and genuinely wanting to be transformed. We need to pray, 'God, I praise you that you forgive all my sin through the death of Jesus. I'm aware of sinful attitudes in my heart and character that contradict being led by your Spirit. Please continue to convict, change and renew my heart and mind in these areas so that I love you and others.'

Spiritual fellowship

Positively, the Holy Spirit gives us opportunities to protect and care for each other. He brings mutual accountability and help:

> Brothers, if someone is caught in a sin, you who are spiritual should restore him gently. But watch yourself, or you also may be tempted. Carry each other's burdens, and in this way you fulfil the law of Christ.
>
> (Galatians 6:1–2)

This is a description of true fellowship. Much that passes as fellowship among Christians is a pale reflection of this. For some people the very idea that wise Christians will be able to help restore others is an appalling thought: 'I am *never* going to let anyone see my sin or try to restore me! How humiliating! I don't need anyone to help me like that!' When we think like this, we miss out on the gentle encouragement of others and the gentle encouragement of the Spirit. We are intended to carry each other's burdens. When we refuse to carry other people's, or let them carry ours, we become fellowship-starved, and our churches can become arid deserts devoid of genuinely spiritual companionship.

A while ago I spoke at an evangelistic discussion event. At the end of the evening a Buddhist medical student said to me: 'I've been at med. school for three years. I disagree strongly with what you said, but I wanted to tell you that in three years this is the first conversation I've had with anyone at all about anything that really matters in life.' Loneliness and lack of community is a tragedy of Western individualism. I was very sad for him, but I am much sadder when I see a similar individualism at work in churches. We have been born again into a body, a new family, a community of the Spirit. Our responsibility to serve others in love, in the Spirit, involves really getting our hands dirty to carry the burdens of other Christians and involves being vulnerable enough to allow others to do so for us.

Gifts for serving in love

The Spirit also gives gifts to Christians for serving each other in love. Consider the following verses from 1 Corinthians:

There are different kinds of gifts, but the same Spirit. There are different kinds of service, but the same Lord. There are different kinds of working, but the same God works all of them in all men.

Now to each one the manifestation of the Spirit is given for the common good.
(1 Corinthians 12:4–7)

Follow the way of love and eagerly desire spiritual gifts . . .
(1 Corinthians 14:1)

Gifts are for serving the body of Christ. 'Different kinds of gifts' equals 'different kinds of service'. Spiritual gifts are gifts from the Holy Spirit, not primarily for personal enjoyment (though there is great joy in exercising them), but for serving each other. We see that in the comparison between 1 Corinthians 12:7 and 14:1 (see Table 2).

1 Corinthians 12:7		1 Corinthians 14:1
The manifestation of the Spirit	equals	spiritual gifts to be eagerly desired
given for the common good	equals	follow the way of love

Table 2

All spiritual gifts are given for the common good, which means that we should eagerly desire them and want to use them in loving service. We fail to serve each other in love if we deny the Spirit gives gifts, if we use them merely for our own satisfaction or if we refuse others the opportunity to exercise their gifts. If we act in any of these ways, we are not being led by the Spirit and our churches and fellowships suffer. Paul insists:

Since you are eager to have spiritual gifts, try to excel in gifts that build up the church.
(1 Corinthians 14:12)

We must not believe the myth that we can be individual, lone Christians, with no contact or fellowship with others. Our readiness to serve should not depend on whether we think there is something in it for us. There is depth and joy and life to serving in the Spirit. Let's not settle for less.

How do we grow in holiness and count ourselves dead to sin?
When speaking about grace I am often asked:

- If the law reveals God's standards of holiness and obedience, aren't you saying that holiness is unimportant?
- Doesn't teaching grace downplay sin and give licence for immorality?'

These are huge and important questions. The answer to both is 'NO!' Holiness is vital, the process of growing in holiness (sanctification) is overwhelmingly important, and sin is dreadfully serious.

I want to show two things. First, that it is not obeying the law that brings sanctification for Christians, but rather living by the Spirit; and secondly, how we grow in holiness through the Holy Spirit.

Paul was asked similar questions because his teaching on justification was so radical. Romans 3 – 5 makes the case that we are justified by faith, through God's grace, not by any work and not by the law. Paul concludes that grace reigns supreme, and that by receiving grace Christians reign in life through Jesus:

> The law was added so that the trespass might increase. But where sin increased, grace increased all the more, so that, just as sin reigned in death, so also grace might reign through righteousness to bring eternal life through Jesus Christ our Lord.
>
> (Romans 5:20–21)

> For if, by the trespass of the one man [Adam], death reigned through that one man, how much more will those who receive God's abundant provision of grace and of the gift of righteousness reign in life through the one man, Jesus Christ.
>
> (Romans 5:17)

Notice the comparison in the second verse. The sin of Adam brings death for all. But where we might expect it to say, 'sin brought death but *our obedience* brings life', it doesn't. It says that God's abundant provision of grace and the gift of righteousness brings life through Jesus.

Lowering the bar?

People instantly accused Paul of lowering the bar on holiness. It is a big enough accusation to merit the whole of Romans 6 and 7 being written to address the question. The questions being responded to are noted in Romans 6:1–2, 15 (see also 7:7, 13):

- 'What shall we say, then? Shall we go on sinning, so that grace may increase? By no means!'
- 'What then? shall we sin because we are not under law but under grace? By no means!'

The implication of the second question is that if the law doesn't condemn us for wrongdoing, then we can sin as much as we wish. We can do whatever we like because it no longer has any consequences. The assumption behind the first question is even worse: if sin brings grace (which is a good thing) and if where sin increases grace increases even more, then why not sin abundantly in order to experience maximum possible grace?!

If you believe the law curbs and inhibits sin, and that replacing law with grace means that there is total freedom, even encouragement, for maximum sinfulness, then you will be very worried about a lot of this book! The false assumption is that the law curbs sin. Paul is very clear that it doesn't – in fact it *increases* it (Romans 5:20). The popular idea that we can measure Christlikeness or our success at holiness through our level of conformity to the law is wrong, as is looking to the law for the remedy to spiritual failure. The curbing of sin comes instead through the Holy Spirit. We have already seen in Romans 8:

> For what the law was powerless to do [free me from condemnation
> and the power of sin and death] in that it was weakened by the sinful
> nature, God did by sending his own Son in the likeness of sinful man to
> be a sin offering. And so he condemned sin in sinful man, in order that
> the righteous requirements of the law might be fully met in us, who do
> not live according to the sinful nature but according to the Spirit.
> (Romans 8:3–4)

The law was powerless to inhibit sin, but the Spirit sets us free from the law of sin and death. He does this by taking all Jesus achieved on the cross and applying it powerfully to our lives.

The mistake made by those who said 'We are not under law so we can sin freely' was that they thought that freedom from the law was freedom from *every* controlling influence in life. Complete freedom to do absolutely anything. But, just as those who think that the law inhibits sin are wrong, so are those who think that being under grace is a licence to behave however we like. The fact is that we are not free from every control. We have been released *from* the condemnation and power of the law *in order* to be betrothed to Jesus Christ. We have been released from condemnation, accusation and guilt in order to live by the Spirit:

> But now, by dying to what once bound us, we have been released from the law so that we serve in the new way of the Spirit, and not in the old way of the written code.
> (Romans 7:6)

And again:

> Therefore, brothers, we have an obligation – but it is not to the sinful nature, to live according to it. For if you live according to the sinful nature, you will die; but if by the Spirit you put to death the misdeeds of the body, you will live, because those who are led by the Spirit of God are sons of God.
> (Romans 8:12–14)

An obligation to the Holy Spirit

Those who are led by the Spirit have an obligation to the Spirit. This may sound as if the freedom of grace that we thought we had been given has suddenly been withdrawn, but it hasn't. Try to think of it like this. Suppose I once had a terrible addiction to smoking. Then imagine that, by whatever means, I was set free from my addiction. Am I now free to have a cigarette? The answer is 'No'. Of course I *could* have one. I could go to the newsagents, buy a pack and light up, but if I do, then I lose the freedom from my addiction. To enjoy my freedom from smoking I am obliged not to smoke.

There are two contradictory freedoms in this illustration. The freedom to smoke contradicts the freedom from addiction. Are we set free from sin and law by Christ? Yes! Are we therefore free to sin? No! Because choosing that supposed freedom to sin destroys our new, real freedom in Christ. In fact the freedom to sin is no freedom at all, but bondage and slavery far more serious than a mere addiction to smoking.

We are obliged to put sin to death by the Holy Spirit. What does this mean practically in everyday life? Two Bible passages sum it up helpfully:

> God cannot be mocked. A man reaps what he sows. The one who sows to please his sinful nature, from that nature will reap destruction; the one who sows to please the Spirit, from the Spirit will reap eternal life. (Galatians 6:7–8)

> In the same way [as Christ died for sins and was raised to life], count yourselves dead to sin but alive to God in Christ Jesus. (Romans 6:11)

Sow to please the Spirit and count yourself dead to sin. Do the things that delight God and reject and throw out everything that offends him. Paul gives three practical things to do in Romans 6 and 7, and one more in Titus 2:11: *believe, behave, relate* and *receive.*

- Romans 6:1–14: *Believe* that you are dead to sin, having died with Jesus. *Believe* that you are raised to new life with Jesus. *Believe* that he is your new master and that he is without sin.
- Romans 6:15–23: *Behave* as someone who is a slave, not to sin but to God. Obey all he says in the Bible. Paul thanks God for the Roman believers: 'that, though you used to be slaves to sin, you wholeheartedly obeyed the form of teaching to which you were entrusted. You have been set free from sin and have become slaves to righteousness' (6:17–18). Determine that every one of your actions, as far as possible, will be offered to righteousness and not to sin.
- Romans 7:1–7: *Relate* to God as someone engaged to a new bridegroom – Jesus Christ! Paul says we have a commitment to

Jesus in which we are growing in fruitfulness to him by serving in the way of the Spirit. *Relate* to Jesus in love, in affections, in will and in delight for having such a perfect, heavenly bridegroom! This is living by the Spirit.

- Titus 2 says, 'For the grace of God that brings salvation has appeared to all men. It teaches us to say 'No' to ungodliness and worldly passions, and to live self-controlled, upright and godly lives in this present age . . .' (Titus 2:11–12). *Grace* teaches us to say 'No.' How does it do it? By replacing our desire for sin with stronger desire for God. *Receive* grace. Pray for it every day. Give thanks for it. Yearn to know more of it. This is reigning in life.

This pattern of believe, behave, relate, receive is what it means to live by the Spirit. Life in the Spirit produces internal obedience that is far superior to mere external conformity. It leads us not *into* sin but to *do battle* with it. Freedom from the law, freedom in the Spirit, does *not* lead to lawlessness and more sin. It leads to practical righteousness because of our loving union with Christ. Dying with Christ doesn't make us slaves to sin, but servants of the Spirit as we come alive in him.

Can we measure life in the Spirit by law?

There is one further question: If we are making every effort to count ourselves dead to sin, and the law revealed sin, is it not legitimate for us still to use the law to see how we are doing at living by the Spirit? Would it not be a helpful, practical measuring stick?

The answer is 'No'. Christ is the goal of the law, the reality towards which it pointed in shadow-form. The law was prophetic of Jesus. Therefore it is good and legitimate to look at the law to find something of the glory of Christ reflected there. However, every time we do, it drives us to the gospel, because it reveals that we are law-breakers who need not law for our holiness, but grace. That is how the law may be the servant of Christ – by showing our need for him, by prophesying about him and by displaying his glory.

Looking at the law can never tell us how well we are doing. It can only tell us that we are law-breakers who need grace. It cannot give power to change or repent – it only accuses and condemns. If we think we have to go back to the old lists in order to find out how to serve our heavenly bridegroom, then Romans 7 says we are committing spiritual adultery! It would be madness to go back to our old husband for advice on how to please our new one. That would be like making Christ the servant of the law. It would be like coming to our new bridegroom merely to receive the ability to go back and obey our old husband. That is the wrong way round!

Power through the gospel
The place we go for our life, growth and sanctification is not the law but the gospel. The death of Christ and the work of the Spirit are not meant to provide the power to go back to the old list, only this time getting it right. They free us from the old list to live by the Spirit. John Piper says:

> But for the righteous – for people who have come to Christ for
> justification and come to Christ for the inner spiritual power to love –
> this role of the law [condemning and convicting to bring us to Christ]
> is past. From now on, the place where we seek the power to love is
> not the law of commandments but the gospel of Christ.[1]

We are being sanctified by the *gospel*. The New Covenant in Jesus' blood is far superior to the old one, carved on stone tablets. We are looking to Christ with great confidence, growing in holiness by the Spirit and having his priorities formed in our hearts by faith. He is making us into people who minister in the power of the Holy Spirit who brings all the abundance of life with God:

> You show that you are a letter from Christ, the result of our ministry,
> written not with ink but with the Spirit of the living God, not on
> tablets of stone but on tablets of human hearts. Such confidence as
> this is ours through Christ before God. Not that we are competent
> in ourselves to claim anything for ourselves, but our competence
> comes from God. He has made us competent as ministers of a new
> covenant – not of the letter but of the Spirit; for the letter kills but
> the Spirit gives life.
> (2 Corinthians 3:3–5)

Questions

1. How would you describe your Christian life? Write down some thoughts on paper.
2. Do any of your thoughts reflect the work of the Holy Spirit? How aware are you of *seeking* to be led by the Spirit or have him transform your desires?
3. Refresh your memory about Paul's list of practical things to do to reckon yourself dead to sin: *believe* you are dead, *behave* as though you are a slave to righteousness, *relate* to God as someone who is betrothed to Jesus and *receive* grace to say 'No' to ungodliness. Which of these do you find hardest? Why?
4. Pray about this area during the coming week, asking for help to know God practically and to be led by the Holy Spirit.
5. Memorize Romans 15:13 to help you recall that living by the Spirit is the way to experience joy, peace and hope:

> May the God of hope fill you with all joy and peace as you trust in him, so that you may overflow with hope by the power of the Holy Spirit.

Notes

1 'How to Use the Law Fruitfully to Bear Fruit for God', <http://www.desiringgod.org/library/sermons/01/112501.html>, accessed 21 July 2004 (sermon for 25 November 2001).

Afterword – progress and joy in the faith

The apostle Paul's whole life was dominated by a single passion:

> For to me, to live is Christ and to die is gain.
> (Philippians 1:21)

He tells us what it means in practice for his whole life to resound with this theme. Living for Christ means having a life of fruitful labour for Christ (1:22). This is how he describes that fruitful labour:

> Convinced of this, I know that I will remain, and I will continue with all of you for your progress and joy in the faith, so that through my being with you again your joy in Christ Jesus will overflow on account of me.
> (Philippians 1:25–26)

So 'to live is Christ' for Paul meant living, teaching and encouraging in such a way that the Philippians made progress in their faith and had joy in their faith. These two themes form the backbone of the letter.

Progress in the faith is much more than merely gaining a deeper understanding of the truths of the gospel. Progress is seen in deeper living out of the gospel. Gordon Fee puts it helpfully:

Such progress regarding the faith will manifest itself as their love for one another increases (1:10; 2:2), as in humility they consider the needs of others ahead of their own (2:3–4), as they 'Do everything without complaining or arguing' (2:14) and as they keep focused on the eschatological[1] prize (3:14–21). This is what it means for them to 'continue to work out your salvation with fear and trembling' (2:12).[2]

Joy in the faith (1:25) is joy in Christ Jesus (1:26). If we want the joy that is the passion of Paul's life, then we will saturate ourselves with Christ. This is why Paul tells the Philippians so many times to rejoice in the Lord. 'To live is Christ' *is* to rejoice in the Lord – to magnify, extol and enjoy the glory of God. Paul's keen hope is that the Philippians' joy will increase until it is overflowing, and that he might play a part in that increase. His desire is to produce worshippers, for that is what it means to overflow with joy in Christ.

Paul's exhortation to us is that we live out the gospel more and more deeply and that we glory in Christ. His conviction is that when we do, our joy overflows. I hope this book has encouraged you more to rejoice in the Lord and all he is for you. Living for Christ is worth it. As we do, he receives glory in the world through the lives and witness of overflowing Christians and we can know his joy. Jesus said:

This is to my Father's glory, that you bear much fruit, showing yourselves to be my disciples.

As the Father has loved me, so have I loved you. Now remain in my love. If you obey my commands, you will remain in my love, just as I have obeyed my Father's commands and remain in his love. I have told you this so that my joy may be in you and that your joy may be complete.

(John 15:8–11)

Notes

1 Here 'eschatological' means 'heavenly'.

2 Gordon D. Fee, *Philippians* (IVP, 1999), p. 73.

Further reading

For your encouragement:

John Piper, *Desiring God: Meditations of a Christian Hedonist* (IVP, 1986)

Sam Storms, *Pleasures Evermore: The Life-Changing Power of Enjoying God* (Navpress, 2000)

Terry Virgo, *God's Lavish Grace* (Monarch Books, 2004)

For a more in-depth discussion of law and grace:

Stanley N. Gundry (ed.), *Five Views on Law and Gospel* (Zondervan, 1993)